Untruth

ROBERT J. SAMUELSON

UNTRUTH

Why the Conventional Wisdom

Is (Almost Always) Wrong

NEW YORK

FOR RICHARD,
THE BRAINS OF THE FAMILY

Author's Note

These columns are reprinted mainly as they originally appeared. In a few cases, the headlines have been changed. Either I did not like the original, or it has lost its meaning as the result of the passage of time. When I spotted factual mistakes, in a few instances, I have corrected them or deleted them. In a few other cases, I have altered the wording slightly when phrases seemed particularly awkward. In no cases has the original meaning been changed.

Contents

PART III

ECONOMICS

PART IV

BUSINESS

Introduction

UNTRUTH: A PRIMER

John Kenneth Galbraith, the economist and writer, coined the phrase *conventional wisdom* more than four decades ago in his 1958 bestselling book, *The Affluent Society*. As Galbraith defined it, the conventional wisdom embodied the prevailing set of beliefs about any particular subject or topic. The beliefs didn't have to be correct. They simply had to be widely held and respectable. Since then, the term has gradually filtered into everyday language, and although Galbraith's original meaning has survived, it has also inspired modern variations. Galbraith's conventional wisdom was solid, staid, and pervasive; newer versions often connote what's trendy, intellectually fashionable, or hip. But whether new or old, the conventional wisdom is (as Galbraith noted) frequently wrong.

Sometimes it is the opposite of the truth. More often it is an artful and selective arranging of facts and perceptions that creates a plausible—though misleading—rendering of reality. But it endures because it tells a story that, at one level or another, is appealing. The conventional wisdom draws its power from this ability to fulfill some psychological or political need. Our behavior then reinforces our beliefs. We see what we want to see. We hear what we want to hear. We search for authorities to repeat and strengthen our beliefs and prejudices. "In some measure the articulation of the conventional wisdom is a religious rite," Galbraith wrote. "It is an act of affirmation like reading from the Scriptures or going to church."

Sooner or later, conventional wisdom may change or crumble. But the agents of destruction are rarely logic or persuasion. They are usually circumstances or the force of events. By its nature, the conventional wisdom resists assault by words or argument. People do not like to be disabused of familiar, self-serving, and satisfying ideas. There's a tendency to suppress doubts, dismiss inconvenient inconsistencies, or deny contradictory evidence. What changes people's minds is irrefutable and sometimes harsh experience. Then the conventional wisdom usually falls. But it's not sweet reason that wields the ax.

I know this firsthand. In 1969 I became a newspaper reporter. The job's main appeal (aside from seeing my name in print) was the opportunity to learn about new things and to explain these discoveries to readers. It was an excuse to ask questions usually off limits to ordinary citizens. Always, the quest was "the truth," even if the ultimate truth—often complex, ambiguous, and disputed—might be hard or impossible to locate. When I began a column in 1976, the aim was the same. It was to convey a fuller understanding of some problem or phenomenon. The more I did this, the more I collided with conventional wisdom, because that's where the reporting led. Increasingly, my columns questioned or rebutted conventional wisdom. Some of those columns are collected in this volume.

Nothing I wrote doomed any bit of conventional wisdom. Some prevailing fads have slipped into well-deserved oblivion, but only because events discredited them. In the mid-1980s we were warned that America's "deindustrialization" was making us a nation of low-paid hamburger flippers and laundry workers (see "We're Not a National Laundromat"); the notion couldn't survive the economic boom of the 1990s. Nor could the idea that Japan would overtake us economically outlive Japan's stagnation in the 1990s. But other suspect ideas continue to flourish, apparently impervious to any amount of unfriendly evidence or logic. We're told that wealthy, conservative interests have come to dominate Washington; it isn't true (see "The Stealth Power Brokers"). More recently, the Internet has been touted as one of the greatest advances in technology since printing; the comparison offends history (see "The Internet and Gutenberg").

Of course, not all conventional wisdom is mistaken. If it were, society might begin to unravel. Everyday blunders, based on faulty ideas, would multiply and spread chaos. Still, we succumb to many dubious fads. Why is this? Galbraith provides few clues. In some ways he merely attached a new label to something old: the inertia of beliefs. People cling to what they know and what makes them feel comfortable. Galbraith attributed this to a dislike of too much originality. It's more than that. It's a pragmatic concession to daily living. If we constantly reexamined every belief and assumption, we'd be paralyzed by indecision. We'd routinely ponder and procrastinate. But in our modern media culture, conventional wisdom isn't what it used to be—and therein lies an engine of errors.

For Galbraith, conventional wisdom consisted of vintage ideas. It was like old wine. It had acquired its reputation through constant repetition over many years by countless authorities. Like good wine, it might spoil. Overtaken by events or new knowledge, it might describe a bygone era or an obsolete theory. By contrast, today's conventional wisdom routinely seems to spring from nowhere. Theories—often on subjects that most people hadn't thought about or on which they had few firm views—acquire sudden fashionability and acceptability. They do not age gracefully. They are instantly bottled, heavily advertised, and eagerly sold. Conventional wisdom is less spontaneous and more contrived than before. It's increasingly an act of intellectual or political merchandising.

This helps explain, I think, why so much of it turns out to be superficial, misleading, or dim-witted. These ideas are creatures of personal ambition, group campaigns, political and intellectual agendas. They do not emerge from a dispassionate effort to discover the truth. They are exercises in salesmanship and suffer from all the excesses of salesmanship. People emphasize what makes their case and overlook or minimize what doesn't. Claims are overstated. Evidence is selective. Qualifications are omitted or obscured.

Politics drives much of this. By politics, I do not mean exclusively or primarily Democratic and Republican, liberal and conservative. Today's dominant form of politics is what I call "the politics of problem solving." Every defect in society must somehow be converted into an identifiable "problem" that can then be "solved"—usually by government, but if not, then by "the market" or someone or something else. By and large, Americans are an optimistic and pragmatic people who worship progress. We are wedded to the idea that problems can be solved—and our imperfections thereby reduced. Americans believe, Tocqueville noted, in "the indefinite perfectability of man." We resist the notion that some shortcomings are simply a normal part of life.

This is not, then, a new impulse. But in our era it has become more pronounced. It is constantly fed by advocacy groups, entrepreneurial politicians—candidates and office holders who cannot rely on a strong central party apparatus to get ahead and must increasingly promote themselves—and intellectual elites, of both Left and Right. All preach to the public on everything from government policy to popular culture. We are led to believe that most social and economic problems can be solved and that people's wants can be relieved or satisfied. By the problems they seek to solve, these various advocates, politicians, and idea merchants define themselves. They establish identities, raise their visibility, and assemble constituencies or audiences. Advocacy blurs with self-promotion.

What this process produces is endless exaggeration. A problem cannot simply be modest, inconvenient, unavoidable, or intractable. It must be large, serious, dangerous, intolerable—and solvable. So problems are overstated in their size and significance, as are the powers of proposed solutions. The pursuit of private contributions to finance political campaigns cannot simply be demeaning and sleazy; it must rattle the very foundations of democracy—and be curable by "campaign finance reform," (see "The Price of Politics"). Managed care cannot simply be a new and imperfect approach to delivering health services; it must be a dehumanizing assault on the integrity of modern medicine—and be curable by "health care reform" (see "Myth of the Managed Care Monster"). In the 1990s the Republican takeover of Congress could not simply be a change in political power that would modify the country's direction and political climate. It had to be a full-scale "revolution" that would change politics and life as we know it (see "They Call This a Revolution?").

To some extent, advocacy requires that arguments become morality tales: good guys (or ideas) vs. bad. Heroes and villains create intellectual and political throw-weight so that agendas can be advanced, skeptics discredited, and opponents vilified. In the United States, this sort of crusading finds a willing audience. Beyond optimism—the faith that what's broken can be fixed—lies our missionary heritage. Americans have always imagined themselves as an exceptional and righteous people bent on improving humanity by assaulting bastions of ignorance, corrupt power, or evil. These national characteristics are great virtues. They often imbue us with a constructive innocence: just because something hasn't been done doesn't mean that it can't be done. The faith in progress can produce progress and often has. But some national virtues, when taken to excess, also become national vices (see "The Vices of Our Virtues").

Problem-solving politics is one of those galling mixtures of success and failure. When failed, it leads to conventional wisdom that abounds with simplicities and stupidities, while inspiring "solutions" that sometimes do more harm than good. The problem in health care is not "managed care" but contradictory public demands: we want universal health insurance, absolute autonomy for patients and doctors over treatment—and controlled health costs. No system can simultaneously satisfy these inconsistent demands. (If everyone has insurance for everything—and doctors or patients can order whatever they want—costs will be uncontrolled.) The problem with "campaign finance reform" is that, if taken to its logical conclusion, it would obliterate political free speech. Inconveniently, modern communication (for television, advertising, mass mailings) requires money. If communication isn't speech, what is it? And if people can't spend to advocate political views and support sympathetic political candidates, how "free" are they?

The art of effective advocacy suppresses doubts that would spoil the moral message. Problems would no longer be so simple, solutions no longer so obvious. Conflicts between desirable goals are minimized, as are the practical limits of proposed solutions. We in the press aid the evasion—and sometimes instigate it. As Americans, we share the problem-solving sensibility. Beyond that, we have our own interests. We need to attract and retain audiences. Both our instincts and interests lie in cultivating controversy and conflict. We are usually eager to sign on to moral or political crusades. They're a good story and appeal to our customers. Although this has long been true, new competitive realities have magnified the effect.

Only a few decades ago—in the 1960s—the national news media comprised a small and stable group of organizations: three TV networks (ABC, CBS, and NBC); three newsmagazines (*Time, Newsweek,* and *U.S. News & World Report*); a few newspapers with national stature (*The New York Times, The Wall Street Journal, The Washington Post*) and only one with a national circulation (the *Journal*); and several major news services (the Associated Press, United Press International). This enabled news professionals—editors, reporters—to retain a decisive say over what was and wasn't "news." Their judgments were obviously fallible and not immune to the reigning political or intellectual fashions. But their judgments were largely their own. With stable audiences, the commercial pressures to use the news to attract readers and viewers was modest.

The situation today is entirely different. The proliferation of media is stunning: cable channels (MTV, ESPN, CNN, C-Span); another major TV network (Fox); two more national newspapers (*USA Today* and *The New York Times*); and countless Internet Web sites with news, financial news, medical information, pornography—and much more. No one's audience is any longer secure. When the networks controlled TV, viewers watched nightly news programs (usually slotted at the same time)—or nothing. Now they can click onto cooking, sports, cartoons, movies, travel stories, home shopping. Or they can surf the Net. Network nightly news audiences have plunged. Newspaper readership has declined more slowly—but decline it has.

The upshot is that the people who run the news business have lost power in determining what is and isn't news. Increasingly, readers and viewers define the news by picking and choosing what they want—or deciding that they don't want news at all. This intensifies the demands on editors and reporters to make the news more popular and palatable. There has been a blurring between news and entertainment, as television's values pervade all media. To lure audiences, commentary has become more strident. CNN's *Crossfire* was a bellwether: the political equivalent of pro wrestling. Editorial independence has receded. Editors still decide what's printed or viewed, but if what they do fails in the marketplace, they will be replaced.

Critics of the mass media often complain that domination by a few big corporate giants subordinates news values to profits. The situation, in many respects, is just the opposite. Greater competition has assailed editorial autonomy. The more media giants there are, the more hard-pressed news values have become. When a few giants dominated (the three TV networks being the obvious examples), they could tolerate greater independence from news divisions, precisely because overall profitability was more certain and predictable. By contrast, today's media giants are more numerous and less secure. The ferocious competition for customers emphasizes commercial success and undermines pure editorial values. To some extent, news has been democratized. It has been thrown increasingly to the dictates of the marketplace. This favors an editorial style that emphasizes morality tales of heroes and villains and sharply drawn conflicts—anything that creates a "buzz."

What I am suggesting is that the way we, as a society, increasingly organize and present information leads—systematically and almost predictably—to misinformation. The precarious media and the practitioners of problem-solving politics (politicians, advocacy groups, "talking heads") have entered into a marriage of convenience. There's mutual exploitation to achieve narrow goals: to attain celebrity or notoriety; to advance a political or intellectual agenda; to capture audience and market share. The result is that we are bombarded by a constant stream of problems (some societal, some the extension of personal problems—drugs, illness, marital abuse, stress) and accompanying solutions. Many of the problems are genuine; some of the solutions might actually help. But there is pervasive exaggeration of both problems and solutions, because that's what grabs attention.

I call this process "untruth." It is the common distortion of reality, which is not—however—typically the result of deliberate lies. Rather, it is an ordinary outcome of our political and media democracy. It's what happens when we explore and debate issues that affect us collectively. If we didn't do this, we wouldn't be who we are. By and large, the process is healthy. But it becomes unhealthy when it simplifies our view of reality and romanticizes our power to alter it. For me, these self-serving simplifications and exaggerations have been a fertile field for reporting and commentary. They beg to be elaborated and qualified. I have tried to provide context: to give people a more candid and complete picture of the world about them. What I have concluded is that the conventional wisdom is (usually) wrong, because it is a vehicle for some political agenda or personal ambition.

In practice, I do not believe that any political, social, economic, or ideological group has a monopoly on untruth. You can see the same mechanics operating similarly across the political spectrum and an array of social concerns and claims. Conservatives tend to glorify "markets" even when markets obviously make mistakes (see "The Mysterious Merger Frenzy"). Liberals tend to overstate the corrosive effects of income inequality (see "The Typical Household Isn't"). Environmentalists talk in doomsday terms about the destruction of the planet (see "Don't Hold Your Breath"). Again, the problems are often real, but they need to be presented in the starkest terms to excite interest or buttress proposed remedies.

Although the techniques are widespread, there's a bias in the types of untruths that acquire prominence. These are "liberal" untruths. The main reason is that the "scribbling and chattering class"—reporters, editors, academics, commentators—tend to be more liberal than conservative. Countless surveys have confirmed this for the press. In 1992 almost 90 percent of Washington reporters voted for Bill Clinton, according to one poll. In the country at large, Clinton's popular vote was only 43 percent. A survey of academics (professors at two- and four-year colleges and universities) published in the *Chronicle of Higher Education* finds the following: 5.2 percent consider themselves "far left"; 39.6 percent "liberal"; 37.2 percent "middle of the road"; 17.6 percent "conservative"; and 0.4 percent "far right."

The result is not a conscious alliance between the press and liberal advocacy groups and Democratic politicians. Most reporters and editors (at least of newspapers, newsmagazines, and mainstream television, though obviously not of opinion journals or shows) subscribe to the notion that they ought to be objective and neutral. They are as eager to cover scandals involving liberals as conservatives. They know that most politicians and partisans try to "spin" stories. Few reporters see themselves as passive platforms for someone else's propaganda. We all know that we're prone to being used by "sources." And much of what the press does has little to do with politics or partisanship. We're simply reporting a "good story" or performing the traditional "watchdog" role of government, large institutions, and corporations.

The bias is more subtle. The stories told by liberal politicians and "experts" of all stripes (economists, scientists, doctors, social scientists, educators) find a more sympathetic ear than the stories told by conservatives. The liberals' heroes and villains, their values and beliefs, correspond more closely with the philosophies and prejudices of reporters and editors. What comes from liberal sources seems more credible and relevant. It matches their notions of social conflict and the pursuit of social good. This is not (they think) bias. It's reality. Often they can't imagine things any other way. By contrast, conservatives—or any nonliberals—are often seen as apologists for business and the rich. Or they're stigmatized as uncompassionate and cranky.

My own values (I believe) are fairly mainstream, though others have labeled them too conservative or—less often—too liberal. I believe Big Government has on the whole benefited the nation, but I also think that the expansion of government poses many practical problems and invites abuse. People can be made too dependent on government benefits. Taxes can go too high for our economic health or personal freedom. Although limits are hard to draw, they exist. Similarly, I put a great deal of faith in "markets"—the freedom to determine what we produce, how it's priced, how we save and invest, and where we work—but do not believe that markets are all-knowing or perfect. They make mistakes and require some government oversight and regulation. There's often a fine line between too little and too much.

Finally, I believe in what are sometimes derided as "traditional family values": parental love and discipline by two parents, if possible. With luck, parents can help their children grow to be responsible and self-reliant adults. Parents provide love, small lessons of everyday living, and the knowledge that someone cares. From this crucible can emerge personal competencies and self-confidence. Although parenting is a haphazard undertaking—and there is no guarantee of success—government and social agencies cannot easily substitute for loving and qualified parents (see "What Money Can't Buy"). I have had one wife and three children, now aged ten to fifteen. They are the most important parts of my life.

As journalists, columnists are (I believe) half-breeds. They are neither pure reporters nor, in my view, pure advocates. They ought to combine the two. They ought to blend a point of view and sensibility with their reporting. The greatest danger—a consequence of being too impressed with your own importance—is becoming a self-parody: someone whose views and style are so predictable that they can be easily mimicked. My particular peril is that, by constantly challenging the conventional wisdom, I become reflexively skeptical of any view held by large numbers of people or routinely criticize anything that is new or different. I am aware of the danger but am not always able to rise above it.

Like most journalism, what we write is usually written on deadline. Judgments must be made quickly. They are often wrong. I doubt there are any major columnists who could not be embarrassed by some of their past writings; if there are, I am not among them. I could have stuffed this book with my own blunders. One of my favorite columns coined the concept of "retarded technology"—the opposite of advanced technology. It signified new technologies that create cumbersome and costly ways of doing things that were once done simply and inexpensively. One example was the electronic book, which struck me as an absurd idea when paper books were so convenient. On reflection, I decided not to include that column.

Robert J. Samuelson
September 26, 2000
Washington, D.C.

PART I

AMERICAN HABITS

THE STEADFAST (AND OFTEN SILLY)
AMERICAN CHARACTER

Every so often an item bounces across the Associated Press wire that reminds you how steadfast the American national character is. Here's one (suitably abbreviated) that arrived a few weeks ago:

ROCHESTER, N.H.—An 88-year-old woman made good on her pledge not to pay "one red cent" of a court judgment against her for taking a neighbor boy's kickball away.

Rochester District Court Judge Franklin Jones accepted a check for $30.20 from someone who sympathized with Reba Martineau rather than pressing Martineau herself to pay. Jones could have jailed her for contempt.

Martineau refused to return nine-year-old Gary Campbell's kickball after it went into the yard of her home in a mobile home park in September. She claimed she and other elderly residents had been treated disrespectfully by neighborhood children. The boy's parents filed a small claims lawsuit to get the ball or make her pay for it. After deducting its fees, the court will give the parents, Martha and Wayne Campbell, $9.99 for a new ball.

Wayne Campbell said they went to court to show their son the law cannot be broken.

Now, a lot of folks think the American national character is going to pot. *Time* magazine recently complained in a cover story that we have become a nation of "crybabies." We sue too often. We see ourselves as the "victims" of someone or something else. The editors at *Time* ought to brush up on their history. What they (and many others) deplore is simply the good old American character adapting to modern times. We may not like what we see, but—as the kickball saga will show—it's the way we've always been.

Americans have long lived by two propositions.

Proposition Number One: You're no better than I am.

Equality is our religion, as Alexis de Tocqueville noted. We may not be equal in income, wealth, or talent. But we categorically reject the idea that people are automatically better or worse merely because they belong to some class or group. Tocqueville found that, unlike Europe, there was no natural aristocracy in America. Everyone is supposed to have the same opportunity. This was our national ideal (and mythology) in the 1830s. It remains so today.

Proposition Number Two: You can't do that to me.

Since at least the Boston Tea Party, Americans have resented arbitrary authority. We have the Bill of Rights to define the limits of outside control over individual conduct. We react strongly against what we regard as intrusions into our lives, whether by government, bureaucracy (private and public), or other groups and individuals. Liberals defend "rights." Conservatives exalt "freedom." They're really talking about the same thing.

Let it be said that these have been—and are—sources of American greatness. They nurture love of liberty, a respect for the individual, and a healthy sensitivity to the abuse of power. But these same impulses can get out of hand. Unless somehow tempered, they can lead to absurd and wasteful conflict.

In a more traditional society, Reba Martineau would have received some deference merely because she is 88. Not in America.

The old aren't superior simply because they're old. We won't have an aristocracy of age or anything else. After "Mama" and "dog," American children first learn to say: "It's not fair." They think they're as good as anyone else, and they're encouraged to believe it. Gary Campbell's parents went to court to show him that, before the law, he was equal to anyone.

What the quarrel was about was freedom and rights. Reba Martineau's offense was that she meddled with Gary Campbell's right to play kickball. Gary Campbell's offense was that he threatened Reba Martineau's right to live in peace and quiet. So they had to have a brawl over their respective rights—at society's expense. Of the ultimate penalty ($30.20), only one-third ($9.99) went for the kickball, while two-thirds ($20.21) covered court costs.

This is a small parable for our larger predicament. Lawyers aren't the only reason (or maybe even the main reason) for the litigiousness of American society. Yes, they encourage it, exploit it, and profit from it. But the basic driving forces lie deep in traditional American values. People or groups who feel they've been wronged or abused believe intensely that our system entitles them to retribution. The system is supposed to enforce equality. It is supposed to protect individual rights and freedoms.

What *Time* describes as "victimology"—the idea that your problems are always someone else's fault—derives from the same values. They are a wellspring for economic, social, racial, sexual, and personal resentment. They provide a ready-made escape from individual responsibility. We're all equal, right? Well, if we're not, then why not? Who's to blame? Every group of individuals that's dissatisfied with life looks for the villain who stole the American dream.

These questions are often fair and legitimate. Social conditions constantly change. Our society is and always will be imperfect. It can't improve itself if no one challenges the status quo. Nor is every lawsuit frivolous. But the trouble is that virtuous American values are increasingly unrestrained by custom, tradition, or common sense. In a bureaucratic and legalized society, there are many points for complaint and pressure. Television and print media provide ample opportunity for publicity and self-expression. Almost every-one can go somewhere to pout about something.

What has gotten us into trouble is the boundless belief in our own national rhetoric. Our virtues, when taken to excess, become vices. They breed self-pity, self-delusion, and pointless conflict. The old American character hasn't died. It's just grown a bit silly. Couldn't someone have said: "Gary, apologize to Mrs. Martineau," and "Reba, please give back the ball"?

The Washington Post
August 21, 1991

THE VICES OF OUR VIRTUES

I am proud to be an American; most of us are. Our patriotism is fierce, if often quiet. A recent Gallup poll asked respondents in 16 countries whether they would like to live elsewhere. Americans finished almost last. Only about 11 percent of us would move. By contrast, 38 percent of Britons, 80 percent of Germans, 20 percent of Japanese, and 19 percent of Canadians would. Why, then, are we so mad at our leaders and society? One neglected answer is this: America's glories and evils are tightly fused together.

The things that we venerate about America—its respect for the individual, its opportunity, its economic vitality, its passion for progress—also breed conditions that we despise: crime, family breakdown, inequality, cynicism, vulgarity, and stress, to name a few. Naturally optimistic, Americans reject any connection between our virtues and our vices. We refuse to see, as sociologist Seymour Martin Lipset argues in an important new book, that "seemingly contradictory aspects of . . . society are intimately related."*

* *American Exceptionalism: A Double-Edged Sword* (Norton, 1997).

But they are, and in an election year, the relationship is highly relevant. Only by grasping it can we keep our perspective on the campaign's inevitable excesses. Already we are deluged with anguished analyses of our faults and vast schemes for self-improvement. Both exaggerate our problems and our capacity to cure them; some national conditions aren't easily changed.

The American creed—our distinct set of values—blends freedom, individualism, and egalitarianism. This mix has fired economic advance. Why do we lead the world in computers? The answer is mostly culture. We love to create, experiment, and tinker. We are the land of Apple Computer and Netscape. Every year more than 600,000 new businesses incorporate. We have the largest global pool of venture capital. But the same emphasis on individual striving, success, and liberty can also promote inequality, inhibit social control, and loosen people's sense of communal obligation.

Crime becomes just another path to "making it." Divorce rises if marriage seems to imperil self-fulfillment. Because we worship individual effort, we are more tolerant of failure and inequality than other nations. In 1987 a poll asked whether "government should provide everyone with a guaranteed basic income." Only 21 percent of Americans agreed—about a third of the number of Germans (56 percent) or Britons (61 percent). Naturally, our welfare state palls next to theirs. Nor should we be surprised by these facts:

• *Among advanced societies, we are the richest—and the most unequal.* In 1995 Americans' incomes averaged roughly 20 to 80 percent above those of Europe and Japan. But the richest 90th percentile of Americans have incomes nearly six times higher than the poor at the 10th percentile. In Germany, the same ratio is three to one; in Canada and Italy, it's about four to one.

• *We have the most successful democracy—and among the lowest voter turnouts.* In the Gallup poll, more Americans (64 percent) were satisfied with democracy than people anywhere else. Canadians (62 percent) were closest; Britons (40 percent) and Japanese (35 percent) were well behind. Yet in nonpresidential elections, less than half of eligible Americans vote.

• *Although decidedly moralistic, we have one of the world's most violent societies.* In 1990 the American murder rate was more than twice as high as Germany's and nine times higher than Japan's.

Contradictions abound. "Concern for the legal rights of accused persons and civil liberties in general is tied to opposition to gun control and difficulty in applying crime-control measures," writes Lipset. Naturally, Americans are among the world's most gun-owning peoples. In 1993, 29 percent of U.S. households had handguns, compared with 5 percent of Canadian and 2 percent of Australian.

To some extent, the proof that our virtues and vices are connected comes from abroad, where the advance of American values has created a natural experiment in social change. The loosening of tight social controls in Russia, China, and South Africa has led to more freedom—and crime. In Europe and Japan, prosperity and the celebration of individuality have coincided with more divorce and crime. Between 1970 and 1991, divorce rates rose 40 percent in Germany and 50 percent in Japan (though both remain well below U.S. levels).

The American creed was already well established by the 1830s, when Alexis de Tocqueville first described it. Even in Colonial times, America was less rigid socially than Europe. Land was a great leveler. In America, most farmers owned it; in England, 60 percent of the population didn't. Still, Colonial America brimmed with hereditary privileges and arbitrary power. In a 1992 book, historian Gordon S. Wood of Brown University argued that the decisive break occurred during the Revolution itself, which created a social and intellectual upheaval.*

Loyalists decamped to Canada, which (like Europe) remained a more deferential, communal, and paternalistic society. But in America, the legitimacy of unchangeable social distinctions collapsed. Jefferson said that men would advance based on "virtue and talent" and not on birth. The Revolution "made the interests and prosperity

_____

* *The Radicalism of the American Revolution* (Vintage, 1993).

of ordinary people—their pursuit of happiness—the goal of society and government," wrote Wood.

The resulting mind-set often means disappointment and division. All authority is suspect, because it elevates some over others and triggers an inbred distrust of "aristocracy"—now "elites" or callous CEOs. Popular culture is democratic and, therefore, sometimes shallow and offensive. Talk radio and trash TV are only new expressions of old impulses. Progress is never sufficient, because happiness—though constantly pursued—can never be guaranteed. Politicians fall short of the ideals that we (and they) set: one reason why we attack them even while admiring our system.

The election will expose these contradictions but not dispose of them. It's great to be an American, but we are burdened as well as blessed by our beliefs. That defines the American drama.

Newsweek
March 11, 1996

BOWLING ALONE IS BUNK

Political scientist Robert Putnam of Harvard has had a good run. Once an obscure academic, he wrote a 1995 article that made him a minor celebrity. President Clinton borrowed his ideas for speeches. Lots of newspapers featured his theory. Putnam argues that civic life is collapsing—that Americans aren't joining, as they once did, the groups and clubs that promote trust and cooperation. This undermines democracy, he says. We are "bowling alone"; since 1980 league bowling has dropped 40 percent.

Guess what. It's mostly bunk. Although Americans may be sour, the reason is not that civic life is vanishing. Solitude in sports? No way. Between 1972 and 1990, the number of Americans playing softball (yes, a team sport) rose from 27 million to 40 million, reports the Amateur Softball Association. Since 1967, the number of teams registered in leagues has jumped from 19,000 to 261,000. Bowling, of course, is merely Putnam's metaphor for a broader disengagement from groups like PTAs and the Elks. But the whole theory is dubious.

It aims to explain a "loss of community": a growing feeling of social splintering. Whether this is real is unclear. Since World War II, just when has America been one big happy family? Not in the 1960s, when the country was torn by Vietnam, civil rights, and campus protest. Or in the 1970s, when Vietnam (continuing), Watergate, and double-digit inflation spawned strife. Perhaps, briefly, in the mid-1950s between McCarthyism and, later, *Sputnik* and school desegregation crises.

Our present conflicts are surely genuine. Their central cause, though, isn't a loss of civic life. The "community" of the past was a more compartmentalized and less compassionate society than today's. Blacks were segregated in schools and jobs. Most married women stayed at home. There was little federal "safety net" for the old and poor. The assault on former discriminations, the pursuit of new liberties and more social justice—all these improved life, while also creating new conflicts and problems.

In some ways, Americans mingle across racial, sexual, and ethnic lines more now than ever. But the security of old social and intellectual compartments is gone. Initially, many changes were imagined to foreshadow harmony: everyone would settle into the middle class and find self-fulfillment. In practice, changes also triggered fierce disputes over government's role, women's (and men's) "rights," gay "rights," and abortion, to name a few.

Groups often reflect and sustain society's stresses and strains. The Ku Klux Klan didn't promote trust; many groups today are agents of discord, not cooperation. Moreover, Putnam wildly exaggerates any decline in group participation. He says that membership in groups like the Red Cross and labor unions has "slumped 25 to 50 percent in the last two to three decades." Okay. But time passes; things change. Unions declined because the economic and legal climate turned hostile. Other groups expanded.

To refute this, Putnam says the General Social Survey—an annual poll of the National Opinion Research Center (NORC) at the University of Chicago—confirms a 25 percent drop in all group membership since 1974. Not really. Putnam's sharp drop occurs only after he makes a statistical adjustment for rising educational levels. In the past, better-educated people have belonged to more groups. Because group joining hasn't risen with rising schooling, Putnam finds a startling "decline."

This is mostly an illusion. The NORC asks respondents whether they belong to 16 types of groups. Here are the raw participation rates for each in 1974 and 1994 (in some cases another year is given, because 1974 or 1994 seems high or low):

Fraternal Groups: 1974, 13.9 percent (1975: 10.9 percent); 1994, 10.1 percent.

Veterans Groups: 1974, 9 percent; 1994, 7.8 percent.

Labor Unions: 1974, 16.5 percent; 1994, 11.8 percent.

Political Clubs: 1974, 4.5 percent; 1994, 4.7 percent.

Sports Clubs: 1974, 17.9 percent; 1994, 21.8 percent.

Youth Groups: 1974, 10.5 percent; 1994, 10.4 percent.

School Groups: 1974, 17.7 percent (1975: 14.1 percent); 1994, 16.1 percent.

Hobby Clubs: 1974, 9.8 percent; 1994, 9.2 percent.

Fraternities: 1974, 4.7 percent; 1994, 5.7 percent.

Nationality Groups: 1974, 3.6 percent; 1994, 3.5 percent (1993, 4.8 percent).

Service Clubs: 1974, 9 percent; 1994, 10.1 percent.

Farm Groups: 1974, 4.3 percent; 1994, 3.7 percent.

Literary/Art Groups: 1974, 9.4 percent; 1994, 9.8 percent.

Professional Groups: 1974, 13.2 percent; 1994, 18.7 percent.

Church-Related Groups: 1974, 42.1 percent; 1994, 33.4 percent.

Other: 1974, 10.4 percent; 1994, 10.7 percent.

There have been some increases; most declines are modest. Church-related groups are the one exception. That lends some weight to Putnam's thesis. But the idea that there's been a massive retreat from civic life is farfetched, as the Reverend Andrew Greeley of the NORC argues. He cites other surveys showing that volunteering actually rose a quarter since the early 1980s. The increase occurred among "Baby Boomers . . . and Generation X," who are stigmatized as being "selfish and uncommitted," he writes.

Americans haven't become recluses. In earlier eras, many social clubs "were a diversion after a horrible workday" in factories, novelist William Kennedy—a chronicler of working-class life—told Peter Hong of the *Los Angeles Times*. And many old social groups, Kennedy noted, reflected prejudice. "The Catholics couldn't join the Protestant groups and the Jews couldn't join any of them," he said.

Hong visited bowling alleys in California and found them thriving. True, leagues had declined, because some teams were organized around plants that had closed. But "almost nobody bowls alone . . . the centers are filled with office parties, rollicking retirees and bowling birthday parties." Hong found no "dearth of community," but rather "more relaxed, less traditional patterns of social connection shaped by the new ways Americans live and work." That's America. "Bowling Alone," by contrast, is mostly about intellectual and journalistic superficiality.

The Washington Post
April 10, 1996

THE TROPHY SYNDROME

The school board of Fairfax County, Va.—a suburb of Washington, D.C.—had a problem: complaints from high school students and principals that class rankings were unfair. On a grade scale of 0 to 4, a majority of students had averages of 3.0 (B) or better. Yet many students were naturally ranked in the lower half of the class. The solution: Eliminate rankings.

We inhabit a self-congratulatory society in which we constantly reassure each other how well we're doing. You can't tell anyone anymore that they're no good—or less good than their peers. We devise artful titles to create the impression that everyone occupies a position of respect and responsibility. *The New Yorker* once ran a cartoon of a man pouring out his woes to a bartender. "I don't know, Al," he says. "On the one hand, there's no doubt that it's a make-work, dead-end job, but, on the other hand, it's also a vice presidency."

My son Michael, six, plays in a soccer league. The highlight of the fall and spring seasons is the same: the trophies. Every team gets trophies. Everyone on every team gets trophies. It doesn't matter whether you finish 9–0 or 0–9. It doesn't matter how well you play or even whether you play. Just show up for the last game, when trophies are distributed. (I can't write "awarded.") Michael has four.

Titles? In Standard & Poor's, I flip to Comerica, Inc., a medium-size bank holding company. It lists one chairman, two vice chairmen, two executive vice presidents, 24 senior vice presidents, and 22 first vice presidents. The press excels at title pollution. Consider *Newsweek*. We have an editor in chief, an editor, a managing editor, four assistant managing editors, 15 senior editors, 20 senior writers, 23 general editors, and 17 associate editors. Many "editors" don't edit. They write; some don't do that. All the titles are meant to sound impressive, even at the expense of honesty. I'm one of ten contributing editors, though I don't edit anything, and some even doubt whether I contribute.

One way to view this rampaging flattery is as constructive hypocrisy: hypocrisy, because we know it's false; constructive, because the pretense does us good. Not everyone can win every game, so we devise consolation prizes that make the losers feel better without hurting the winners.

After all, my son plays in games where score is kept. Who cares if losers get trophies, too? (For the record, Michael's team—the Big Birds—finished 5-2-2.) Not every rising manager can be a CEO. So what if the also-rans proliferate into vice presidents? Sociologist Harriet Zuckerman of Columbia University reports that the United States now has roughly 3,000 major scientific prizes, five times as many as 20 years ago. But she doubts that work effort or the ardor for discovery have suffered just because prizes are easier to win.

In a recent book, economist Robert Frank of Cornell University argued that many of these accommodations make perfect sense.* People value status, and we find new ways to create it or to keep content those who have less of it. Fancy job titles provide psychic income. The welfare state enables those on top to stay there by making life on the bottom a little more tolerable.

---

* *Choosing the Right Pond: Human Behavior and the Quest for Status* (Oxford University Press, 1985).

Vicious competitiveness, unless checked, can be ugly and socially destructive. Do we really want a country of John McEnroes? The reasoning that persuaded the Fairfax School Board to allow schools to drop class rankings was simple. Many grades were bunched together. Rankings were artificial (students with similar grades might have wildly divergent ranks) and, therefore, were unfair. Low ranks were hurting students' college admissions.

"Kids shy away from demanding courses or demanding teachers, because it will affect class rank," says principal Joseph Arangio of Langley High School. A student in a neighboring county told *The Washington Post:* "I know people who sat down and cried when they got their rank. They said, 'I worked so hard, and this is what I have to show for it.' People flip out over these things."

Up to a point, all this rings true. But perhaps you suspect (as I do) that things have gotten out of hand. Competition can be nasty, but it's often useful. "No pain, no gain" is usually true. Even before clichés like this, Edison said: "Genius is 1 percent inspiration and 99 percent perspiration." The tendency to tell everyone that everything is okay—everyone gets a trophy—may temporarily lower stress, but it relaxes the pressure to do our best, which may be better than we thought we could do.

People suppress bad news. By now it is well known that U.S. students score poorly in many international comparisons—but rate themselves near the top. Doubtlessly, the executives who mismanaged General Motors convinced themselves that they were doing fine. One reason class rank may now make less sense than in the past is grade inflation. In 1966, 15 percent of college freshmen had A averages in high school. By 1991, that was 24 percent.

This sort of socially acceptable self-deceit is designed to spare hurt feelings and puff up our self-esteem. But it's harmful when the truth ultimately intrudes, as it usually does. It did at GM. Schools can end rankings and give everyone A's. But they can't create more openings at elite colleges to which their students aspire. Students who expect to get in won't. Handling disappointment—and going on from it—is one of life's lessons. It is taught by experience, not denial. Too much self-satisfaction tempts us to treat disappointment as somebody else's fault. Because we're okay, blame for our misfortune must lie elsewhere.

It's also clear that constructive hypocrisy is often plain old hypocrisy. It breeds cynicism and waste. Too many vice presidents create bureaucratic bloat. The cavalier use of inflated titles substitutes for imaginative management that enables people to make genuine contributions. Making high school and college degrees easier to get causes many people to differentiate themselves by pursuing less common "higher" degrees. Hence, the growth of "credentialing": an explosion of master's and professional degrees, many of dubious value.

Everyone likes praise. At the age of six, an extra pat on the back is helpful. A few trophies are no big deal. Our problem is that we perpetuate childish customs. Praise given too easily or too lavishly is worse than none. Trophies are worth something only if they are earned, not bestowed.

Newsweek
December 21, 1992

THE LAST DAD TO VISIT
DISNEY WORLD

I recently became the last dad in America to visit Disney World in Orlando. This is spiritually, if not precisely, true. Considering the circumstances (three children, aged five to ten, adequate income, East Coast residence), I was doomed to go. And a good thing, too, because—journalistically speaking—Disney World is not to be missed. In many ways it is what modern America is about. It expresses our conviction that technology and management can maximize fun and advance "the pursuit of happiness."

At Disney World, everybody is supposed to have a good time and get along. It is a self-contained community in which all social conflict and family strife are officially banished. Everything is organized and almost regimented. There's a monorail and a fleet of more than 100 buses to transport the massive crowds. In 1994 attendance totaled 29 million, reports *Amusement Business,* a trade publication. Even with double counting (customers who made many visits), that's a lot of people.

A friend of mine thinks that Disney World is the ultimate reason we won the cold war. He could be right. The promise of American life—the promise projected to the world for the past half century—is that democratic capitalism would not simply free people from tyranny, but also deliver them to self-fulfillment. We can be liberated from poverty by economic growth and transported to pleasure. Disney World epitomizes that idea.

Gosh, it's big. Here are some indicators. The Disney property is 43 square miles, which (as the promotional literature says) is twice the size of Manhattan. On this property are three theme parks (the Magic Kingdom, Epcot, and the Disney-MGM Studios), three water parks, five golf courses, 23 hotels and resorts with 22,000 rooms, and a gazillion stores. With only a third of the land developed, there's room for growth. A fourth theme park (Wild Animal Kingdom) is scheduled to open in 1998.

The stores are crammed with T-shirts, stuffed animals, coffee cups, videotapes, hats, shorts, slippers—almost anything that can be tied to Disney or the parks. In one store (the Art of Disney), a bronze statue of Goofy sells for $10,500, and a Mickey Mouse leather armchair costs $3,400. People used to wonder where, as automation eliminated factory jobs, Americans would work. One answer is the entertainment-industrial complex—everything from TV to tourism to pro football to amusement parks. All told, Disney World employs 37,000. (To put that in perspective: Microsoft Corp. has only 17,800 workers.)

Disney World, opened in 1971, caps a century of growth in commercial leisure. "In the 1870s and 1880s, 'night life' was still the preserve of the wealthy few who patronized the first-class playhouses and of the 'sporting crowd' that spent its evenings in 'concert' saloons with live entertainment," writes historian David Nasaw of the City University of New York. But soon, "the landscape of amusements . . . changed dramatically."

By 1910, according to Nasaw, New York's playhouses and movie theaters could seat two million people. In 1870, there were no public amusement parks or baseball parks. Three decades later, "there were enclosed baseball and amusement parks" in most major cities and many towns. In 1909, 20 million people played and swam at

Coney Island in New York. "A working man wants something besides food and clothes in this country," a printer testified to a Senate committee in 1883. "He wants recreation."

So it was then—and still is. Regardless of how long you stay (and we stayed a week; it was our only summer vacation), you can't do everything at Disney World. We rode the Big Thunder Mountain Railroad, Splash Mountain, and Space Mountain. We did the Tower of Terror. We swam at two water parks, had two "character" breakfasts (with Disney figures like Mickey Mouse), saw two 3-D movies, and took Mr. Toad's Wild Ride. My ten-year-old daughter kept a running tally; by her count, we did 48 rides, parades, exhibits, and events.

Of course, the fantasy and its realization are not always the same. Among other things, Disney World has inspired travel guides. The one we used (*The 1995 Unofficial Guide to Disney World*) contained this cautionary letter from a mother in Dayton, Ohio, who had visited with her five-year-old daughter:

> By 11 in the morning we had walked so far and stood in so many lines that we were all exhausted. Kristy cried about going on anything that looked or even sounded scary. . . . We got hungry about the same time as everyone else, but lines for food were too long and my husband said we would have to wait. By one in the afternoon we were just plugging along, not seeing anything we were really interested in, but picking rides because the lines were short or because it was air-conditioned.

This, too, is reality. Many parents and children get on each other's nerves; perhaps all do. The American Dream never quite lives up to its billing; so, too, Disney World. The *Unofficial Guide* observes: "Few humans (of any age) . . . are mentally or physically equipped to march all day in a throng of 50,000 people, not to mention the unrelenting Florida sun." Waits can be demoralizing, though ours weren't. Through infinite twists, Disney compresses long lines into small spaces.

Still, the throngs continue. In 1994, the Disney Co. collected $3.5 billion from all its theme parks, which also include the original Disneyland in California and a park in Japan. (EuroDisney is a separate company.) The crowds are no elite: they are a fairly wide sampling of America. I'm not sure whether this is a triumph of commercial democracy or a sign of encroaching decadence. Disney World has two shows on America itself, and in one, someone stuck in this subversive quote from John Steinbeck: "We now face the danger which in the past has been the most destructive to [nations]. Success, plenty, comfort, and ever-increasing leisure: no dynamic people have ever survived these dangers."

At Disney World, that's a party stopper. Are we condemned by our own success? You think about it; I didn't. Disney World is no place for reflection. Too much to do. The children enjoyed themselves, despite some rough spots. So did my wife. It was hard not to have fun, even though I tried.

The Washington Post
September 13, 1995

AMBITION AND ITS ENEMIES

We are a nation of ambitious people, and yet ambition is a quality that is hard to praise and easy to deplore. It's a great engine of American creativity, but it also can be an unrelenting oppressor that robs us of time and peace of mind. Especially in highly prosperous periods—periods like the present—it becomes fashionable to question whether ambition has gotten out of hand and is driving us to excesses of striving and craving that are self-destructive.

Ambition is not, of course, only a quest for riches. The impulse pervades every walk of life. Here is Al Gore straining to be president—campaigning earnestly without any apparent joy—to fulfill an ambition that must date to his diaper days. And does anyone really believe that the fierce rivalry among America's immensely rich computer moguls (from Microsoft's Bill Gates to America Online's Stephen Case) is about money? What it concerns is the larger ambition to control the nation's cyberagenda.

One-upmanship is a national mania. You see it every time a wide receiver prances into the end zone and raises his index finger in a triumphant "We're number one" salute, even if his team is mired in a losing season. More common is the search for status symbols—a bigger house, a more exotic vacation, a niftier bike, a faster computer—that separate us from the crowd. Money may not be the only way to satisfy this urge, but it's the most common because it can so easily translate itself into some other badge of identity and standing.

For many people, the contest seems futile. *The New York Times* recently ran a long story on four families with roughly $50,000 of income "who wonder why they have to struggle so hard just to pay the bills." The answer isn't that their incomes are stagnating. Between 1992 and 1997, the median income of married couples rose from $48,008 to $51,681 in inflation-adjusted dollars, reports the Census Bureau. They are surely higher now [1999]. All the families profiled by the *Times* owned homes. Their recent purchases included "double-door refrigerators, radiant-heat stoves . . . big-screen TVs . . . computers, and elaborate outdoor grills."

The problem isn't that they're running in place, but that they're running in the pack with everyone else. Consumer products morph from luxury to convenience to necessity. Cars, TVs, and microwaves all followed the cycle; now it describes Internet connections and cell phones. If you don't buy by the final stage, you're considered a crank or a pauper. There's nothing new here. In *The Theory of the Leisure Class* (1899), Thorstein Veblen argued that once an item becomes widely owned, possessing it becomes a requisite for "self-respect." People try to consume "just beyond [their] reach" so they "can outdo" those with whom they compare themselves.

Frustration is preordained. Despite the booming economy, a *Newsweek* poll in June reported that 29 percent of adults found it more difficult to live the kind of life they want, while only 23 percent found it less difficult. (For 47 percent, there was no change.) The stress can lead to tragedy. Perhaps this is the story of Mark Barton, the day trader who murdered 12 people. People routinely try to beat the system through get-rich-quick schemes. This partly explains the explosion in legalized gambling. In 1998, Americans lost about $50 billion gambling. About 125 million people gamble, and

7.5 million are problem or pathological gamblers, reports the National Gambling Impact Study Commission.

We're constantly advised to subdue ambition. Search for deeper meaning in family, friends, and faith, we're told. Money cannot buy happiness. This seems sensible—up to a point. The General Social Survey at the University of Chicago asks people to rate their happiness. The 1998 survey shows a somewhat stronger relation between money and happiness than earlier polls. About 34 percent of those with incomes between $30,000 and $50,000 were "very happy," and 58 percent were "pretty happy." Above $110,000, the ratings were 51 percent "very happy" and 45 percent "pretty happy." (Marriage has a bigger impact than income; the "very happy" rate of couples is about double that of singles.)

In a recent book (*Luxury Fever*), Cornell University economist Robert Frank urges that we penalize overambition with a progressive consumption tax. The more people spend, the higher their tax rate. Spend $5,000 on a watch instead of $50, and your taxes go up; buy a car for $60,000 instead of $20,000, and pay more taxes. People wouldn't be worse off, Frank argues, because they'd be shielded from the arms race pattern of competitive consumption. Indeed, they'd have more free time, because it wouldn't pay to work so hard.

Hmm. Let's rethink. Though unlovable, ambition is socially useful. It sustains economic vitality. It prods people to take risks and exert themselves. The Internet is the offspring of workaholics spending eight-day weeks to invent a new world and make a fortune. When the process works well, gains overwhelm losses—and not just in economic output. Today's hyperprosperity has improved the social climate. Almost all indicators of confidence have increased.

What people disdain as ambition they also venerate as opportunity. As Tocqueville long ago noted, America was built on the notion that—unlike Europe, with its hereditary aristocracy—people could write their own life stories. The ideal endures. A 1996 survey asked whether anyone starting poor could become rich; 78 percent of

Americans thought so. But it's not just the economy or even politics. Social standing is fluid everywhere. Ambition and its creative powers permeate the arts, the professions, academia, science. Because everyone can be someone, the competition to rise above the crowd is unrelenting and often ruthless.

Few of us escape ambition's wounds. There are damaged dreams, abandoned projects, and missed promotions. Most of us face the pressures of balancing competing demands between our inner selves and outer lives. A society that peddles so many extravagant promises sows much disappointment. Ambition is bitter as often as sweet; but without it, we'd be sunk.

Newsweek
August 23, 1999

FADDISH ATTACKS ON THE
MERITOCRACY

If the Founding Fathers ever envisioned an ideal social order, it was surely a meritocracy: a system under which people succeed mainly on the basis of ability and effort. We are probably closer to that ideal now than ever before. More Americans go further in school, and our best colleges and universities are more open to students of all backgrounds. The executive ranks of business have been similarly, if less decisively, democratized. Yet the meritocracy is now under furious intellectual assault.

The indictment, crudely, is that we are creating a caste society unfairly dominated by upscale snobs. Richer than other Americans, they are increasingly insulated from popular beliefs and tastes (so it's said). Worse, they perpetuate their position by sending their children to elite private universities that are gateways to the best jobs. In a book a few years ago, Labor Secretary Robert Reich called the new upper tier "symbolic analysts." Charles Murray and the late Richard Herrnstein termed it "the cognitive elite" in *The Bell Curve*. And Michael Lind calls it "the over-class" in his book *The Next American Nation.*

As with most stereotypes, this one contains some truth. Managers and professionals—the core of this new class—have exploded. Since 1940 the labor force has slightly more than doubled to 119 million in 1993. Meanwhile, managers quadrupled (from 3.8 million to 15.4 million), and engineers quintupled (from 300,000 to 1.7 million); doctors and lawyers expanded sharply (lawyers went from 182,000 to 777,000 and doctors from 168,000 to 605,000). With more managers and professionals, they can be treated as a cohesive class that can be analyzed, criticized, or satirized.

It's a setup. We don't live in a classless society (and never will), but we do live in an enormously fluid one. That is the central point that all these analyses miss or minimize. The meritocracy is no monolith. It has its own cultural, economic, and political fissures (doctors vs. lawyers on malpractice, for example). And the success of the people at the top does not cause the poverty of the people at the bottom. If elite universities didn't produce successful graduates, you'd wonder: Why not? They do. But if a prestige degree was the only path to advancement, you'd worry: Is America a closed society? It isn't.

One report in the mid-1980s on 2,729 top executives at 208 major corporations found that 17 percent of them didn't go to college or dropped out; an additional 28 percent had bachelor's degrees from nonprestige schools. At *Newsweek,* editor Maynard Parker graduated from Stanford; but his boss, editor in chief and president Richard Smith, went to Albion College. Jack Welch and John Smith, the heads of General Electric and General Motors, both graduated from the University of Massachusetts.

I am not denying the obvious. In life it helps to come from a high-income, well-educated family and to go to a well-known college. But the image of a pampered elite that can easily program its own future is vastly overdrawn. I graduated from Harvard; my father had no college degree. The odds that any of my three children will go to Harvard—assuming they want to—are low; the chances of all of them going are zero. Indeed, elite colleges have become less accommodating of alumni. As late as 1961, almost a quarter of Yale freshmen were sons of Yale College graduates. In 1994, only 9 percent were.

In America, the paths to fame and fortune (and even content-ment) are many and ever changing. Two of the nation's most power-ful men today, Bill Gates and Rush Limbaugh, are college dropouts. People have different talents, ambitions, drives, and luck. Brothers and sisters pursue different life goals with varying success. Nor have those with higher incomes been entirely sheltered from eco-nomic upheaval. Managers and professionals have suffered from "downsizing." By one government study, job security (though still considerable) eroded as much in the 1980s for college as for high school graduates.

It is precisely the realization, among better-educated and higher-income Americans, that they cannot fully guarantee their own fu-tures—let alone their children's—that has raised society's audible anxiety. Down the economic ladder, people have always faced pos-sible layoffs and interrupted incomes. Hardly anyone loudly com-plained. Upscale society imagined itself immune to these possible upsets, and the recognition that this is an illusion has triggered out-cries. But change and insecurity define both a competitive economy and a meritocracy.

Our new class theorists downplay this endless turbulence and, in the process, forget history. In a recent book, the late Robert Christo-pher described the "de-WASPing of America's power elite"—that is, the decline of the stranglehold of white, Anglo-Saxon Protestants on our major business and cultural institutions. Wrote Christopher: "When I left to enter the Army in late 1942, my hometown of New Haven, Connecticut, was a place where marriage between Irish and Italian Americans [still raised] eyebrows on both sides, where social intercourse between WASPs and Italian or Jewish Americans was still minimal and generally awkward, and where no one of Polish or Greek heritage could sensibly hope ever to win the presidency of a local bank or brokerage house."

The social barriers of Christopher's youth have been battered by intermarriage, more education, and new social norms. In 1940, less than 5 percent of Americans had a college degree; now nearly 25 percent of young Americans do. At Yale (whose records are very good), about 70 percent of freshmen came from private schools in 1940. In 1994, nearly 60 percent came from public schools. Almost half were women, first admitted in 1969. About 10 percent were black, 7 percent were Hispanic, and 16 percent were Asian American. Two-fifths received financial aid.

Our meritocracy has flaws and hypocrisies. Doctors, lawyers, and managers often act in self-interested ways, just as unions do. There are advantages of privilege and connections; "affirmative action" is another wrinkle. But whatever its defects, the meritocracy is a huge advance over the preceding barriers of race, sex, religion, and ethnicity. Life is unfair, John Kennedy once said. It always will be—but it is not rigged, at least not in America.

Newsweek
July 31, 1995

GOODBYE, MIKE MULLIGAN

It looks as though my days with Mike Mulligan are finished. Mike is the hero of *Mike Mulligan and His Steam Shovel,* which I've read to our three children. Frankly, I dote on Mike and his shovel, Mary Anne. But John—our youngest, almost five—now rejects the book. John is the most stubborn of the tribe, and when he says no, it would take more than Mike and Mary Anne to budge him. Certainly, I can't. He is, of course, wrong. The book, originally published in 1939, is not just a charming children's story but also a classic American tale. It is Mike's odyssey to spare Mary Anne from obsolescence, as diesel shovels condemn steam shovels to the scrap heap: "All the other steam shovels were being sold for junk, or left out in old gravel pits to rust and fall apart. Mike loved Mary Anne. He couldn't do that to her."

Here are enduring themes: man's emotional bonds with machines; the struggle against adversity; the transforming effects—for good and ill—of new technology. In our times, we think ourselves assaulted by unprecedented forces of trade and business "restructuring." Well, it isn't so. The changes of yesteryear were often more wrenching. Sometimes we need to remember. Virginia Lee Burton (1909–1968), who wrote *Mike Mulligan,* had a genius for reducing these epic upheavals to small sagas of the human spirit.

In *The Little House* (1942), she tells the story of a home built on a secluded hill that gradually becomes surrounded by roads and other homes and, finally, by the trolley tracks and towering apartments of a big city. This story would have been familiar to the parents and grandparents who first read *The Little House.* In their lifetime, America had become a highly urbanized society. Consider Cleveland. In 1860, it had a population of 43,000; by 1930, that was 900,000. Its area exploded from seven square miles to 71. Steel mills and machine shops covered what had been farmland.

Ultimately, the granddaughter of the original builder spots the house and has it moved to a new hilltop far away from the city. Her act is not so much a denial of the city as a reaffirmation of old values. So it is with *Mike Mulligan.* The steam shovel's downfall is but a footnote to the larger story of how electricity and internal-combustion engines replaced steam power. "Throughout the nineteenth century, steam was the wonder energy source," says Bill Withuhn, a curator at the Smithsonian Institution.

Most steam engines operated similarly. Coal was burned, boiling water and producing steam that pushed pistons. In factories, the pistons moved shafts and belts that powered machines that made furniture, clothes, or tools. On farms, steam engines ran tractors; 85,000 were built between 1876 and 1931. And, of course, steam locomotives were one of the last survivors of the steam age. At the end of World War II, railroads had 40,000 of them; by 1960, most had been replaced by 27,000 diesel locomotives.

The diesels had many advantages. Steam engines had to stop every 50 miles for water and every 100 miles for coal; diesels didn't. They had more standardized parts and needed less maintenance. Diesels operated 85 to 90 percent of the time, says Withuhn, compared with 60 to 70 percent for steam locomotives. "The diesel was a lifesaver," one railroad president said. But many managers were "reluctant to get rid of the steam engine. The hard facts can be tough when you're dealing with emotions."

It wasn't, of course, just emotions. Between 1945 and 1962, rail employment fell from 1.4 million to 700,000. Fewer engineers were needed; maintenance shops got smaller; fueling and watering stops were eliminated. Cities like Altoona, Pennsylvania—with massive repair shops—were devastated. Similar forces assailed steam shovels in the 1920s and 1930s. "Diesels were cheaper," says Robert Vogel, an expert on old machines. "There was no water supply [needed] and no ashes to haul out."

A racket: Mike Mulligan was undaunted. He finds that the town of Popperville is planning a new town hall. "We are going to dig the cellar of that town hall," he says. In Popperville, Mike and Mary Anne meet selectman Henry B. Swap. Mike proposes digging the cellar in "just one day" or not be paid. Swap figures that the job is impossible and that the town can get something for nothing. So, he smiles "in a rather mean way" and says okay.

What a contest. Steam shovels made a racket. They belched out smoke and steam. They creaked and groaned. Part of their romance was that everyone could see how they worked. Gears and cables were highly exposed. As Mike and Mary Anne begin, a crowd gathers to cheer them. The more people watch, the "faster and better" they dig. The phone operator (this predates long-distance dialing) helps. She calls "the next towns of Bangerville and Bopperville and Kipperville and Kopperville and told them what was happening in Popperville. All the people came over to see if Mike Mulligan and his steam shovel could dig the cellar in just one day."

As the sun sets, Mary Anne scoops out the last bucket of dirt. Everyone claps until someone notices that there's no ramp to get out of the cellar. Mike and Mary Anne are stuck. Henry B. Swap smiles "in a rather mean way" and says they won't be paid. No one knows what to do until a boy suggests building the town hall over Mary Anne: Let her be the boiler and Mike be the janitor. It's settled: Even Swap agrees.

And so, Americans triumph over adversity and embrace change. The struggling is necessary, even if all stories don't end happily. We are inspired and reminded that upheavals today, though imposing, are less daunting than in the past. Meanwhile, Mike and Mary Anne remain in Popperville. They invite anyone passing through to visit. Until then, bye, Mike.

Newsweek
December 19, 1994

DEMOCRACY IN AMERICA

Alexis de Tocqueville (1805–1859) wouldn't have been surprised by the campaign's bitterness, with one candidate (Gore) cast as a liar and the other (Bush) as an imbecile. Tocqueville would have had an interesting explanation because, even though he was French, he understood the United States as well as anyone, before or since. His *Democracy in America* remains the "best book ever written on democracy and the best book ever written on America," say political scientists Harvey C. Mansfield and Delba Winthrop in their major new translation.* Its appearance is fortuitous: an opportunity—just as the campaign ends—to assess why American democracy succeeds, despite its many shortcomings.

Tocqueville arrived in the United States in 1830 in his mid-twenties. He stayed nine months and traveled widely to Boston, Buffalo, Pittsburgh, Memphis, New Orleans, Washington, and the then frontier areas of Michigan and Wisconsin. He talked to President Andrew Jackson, ex-president John Quincy Adams, Daniel

---

* *Democracy in America* (University of Chicago Press, 2000).

Webster, and many others. Tocqueville aimed to see what might await France, which, despite its revolution, remained bitterly divided over democracy's value. "I wanted to . . . know at least what we ought to hope or fear from [democracy]," he writes.

What he discovered was that America's democracy was not just government and politics. It was a set of beliefs, values, and practices about what people should expect from life. Consider his opening lines:

> Among the new objects that attracted my attention during my stay in the United States, none struck my eye more vividly than the equality of conditions. I discovered without difficulty the enormous influence that this primary fact exerts on the course of society; it gives a certain direction to public spirit, a certain turn to the laws . . . it creates opinions . . . and modifies everything.

In *Democracy in America*—published in two volumes, in 1835 and 1840—Tocqueville showed how this new American sensibility permeated society, from politics to poetry. What he meant by "equality of conditions" was closer to our "equality of opportunity" than to "equality of results." It was, he writes, "the right to indulge in the same pleasures, to enter the same professions . . . to live in the same manner and pursue wealth by the same means."

Here was America's novelty—the assumption that no one was automatically superior to anyone else. This separated America from the Old World, with its aristocratic heritage. Property there was mainly inherited, not acquired. Social and economic standing flowed heavily from birth, not talent or labor. People knew their place. "Tocqueville always understands democracy in contrast to aristocracy," write Mansfield and Winthrop. The two were "opposed ways of life."

The American sensibility altered family relations. Even then, women's roles—compared with those in Europe—expanded. Art tended toward "the quickest or the cheapest," because no longer were there only a few wealthy patrons as buyers. Above all, Americans were ambitious and acquisitive. Tocqueville recognized how the appetite for equality bred materialism, which, far from satisfying people, made them more anxious:

> It is a strange thing to see with what sort of feverish ardor Americans pursue well-being and how they show themselves constantly tormented by a vague fear of not having chosen the shortest route that can lead to it. . . . In addition to the goods that [the American] possesses . . . he imagines a thousand others that death will prevent him from enjoying if he does not hasten.

What's astonishing is that Tocqueville extracted these conclusions from a country that seems so far removed from our own. In 1830 the United States had slightly less than 13 million people. There were only 24 states (the last, Missouri, had been admitted in 1821) and almost no railroads (the first three-mile line was built in 1826). Tocqueville's insights confirm his brilliance and remind us that many features of national character are virtually indestructible.

Though admiring of America, Tocqueville was hardly uncritical. Democratic values, he thought, often encouraged conformity. He scathingly described the treatment of Native Americans and felt that slavery might lead to a race war. As for politics, he noted that elections inspired "intrigues" and "agitation." He may have understated the case. In a recent book, historian Joyce Appleby of UCLA shows that early-nineteenth-century politics could be incredibly bitter.* The split between Federalists (the party of John Adams) and Republicans (the party of Thomas Jefferson) was poisonous. Duels remained a way of settling scores. Writes Appleby: "Andrew Jackson . . . slew a young political opponent in cold blood. The man, having grazed Jackson in a first shot, had to stand at the mark while Jackson recocked his gun." (Now, that's the politics of personal destruction.)

But the defects of politics weren't crippling, because American democracy didn't depend exclusively on politics and government

---

* *Inheriting the Revolution* (Harvard University Press, 2000).

for its vitality. There were other outlets for democratic energies. Commerce had huge appeal. Civic associations of various sorts abounded. Religion—again, in many varieties—flourished. The country's sheer size offered ample opportunities. This was one of Tocqueville's central messages: Democracy could succeed in America because its passions could be absorbed in many different ways. Politics and government were important, but they weren't the only things that were important. Disappointments and disagreements might not be fatal because people could pursue their ambitions and practice their values in many realms.

There was a big caveat, however. Tocqueville worried that the obsession with individuality might become self-defeating selfishness. If people thought only of themselves and their families, they might be so disengaged that they became vulnerable to the "despotism" even of a democratic government. Like many of Tocqueville's insights, this one remains relevant.

Newsweek
November 13, 2000

PART II

POLITICS

THE VIRTUES OF GRIDLOCK

Everyone deplores political "gridlock" these days. Both *The New York Times* and *The Washington Post* have run long articles stigmatizing divided government (Republican White House/Democratic Congress). President Bush urges voters to end the deadlock by electing a Republican Congress; Bill Clinton makes the same pitch with the party label reversed. David Broder of the *Post,* the nation's best-known political reporter, states flatly that "divided government is not working. Only the votes can fix this mess by voting straight tickets in November."

Count me out. I love divided government.

For all its flaws, it protects us against the worst excesses of both parties. Frankly, the specter of President Clinton wheeling and dealing with a Democratic Congress rattles me. Clinton believes in activist government, and Congress instinctively panders to its many constituencies. The logic of this combination is an explosion of government spending, regulation, and special-interest legislation. There would be no discipline (the threat of a presidential veto) to stop it.

Republican government might be worse. Arguably, it might show more budgetary restraint, despite the GOP's public enthusiasm for tax cuts. But what's scary is the Republican's intolerant, even hateful, social agenda. Their moralism—on abortion, school prayer, and family affairs—says: Let us impose our values on you. Although not all Republicans feel this way (just as not all Democrats want more spending), a Republican government would face intense partisan pressure to use federal power to promote values not shared by most Americans. The prototype: the ban on abortion counseling in federally funded clinics.

Give me divided government any day.

The false appeal of one-party government lies in a simple model of how politics should operate. By this view, each party has a clear-cut program. Voters pick one or the other. The winning party adopts its program. Voters scrutinize the results and decide whether to re-elect the incumbents. Voters have real choices, and parties are rewarded or punished on the basis of performance.

By contrast, divided government is said to promote political irresponsibility and public cynicism. Because no single party controls everything, each can conveniently blame the other for the nation's problems. The results are portrayed as immense budget deficits, runaway health costs, and a feeble economy. The public feels powerless and grows disaffected with national leadership and institutions.

The trouble with this neat analysis is that it doesn't reflect the way our politics actually work or, in my view, the way they should work. There are two misconceptions:

1. Divided government produces legislative paralysis (AKA gridlock). This is flat wrong. Contrary to popular wisdom, the Bush years are full of major legislation. To wit: the Americans with Disabilities Act (creating new rights for the disabled), the Clean Air Act of 1990, the Civil Rights Act of 1991, the budget agreement of 1990, the S&L bailout law. In addition, the White House and Congress have agreed to scale back the military by about 25 percent. My point is not to praise or damn these actions. It is merely to show that the perception of paralysis is vastly exaggerated.

Recent experience is typical. In a study, Yale political scientist David Mayhew found that divided governments consistently enact major laws. For example, the Nixon administration produced the Clean Air Act of 1970 and the Occupational Safety and Health Act. It created the Consumer Product Safety Commission and Amtrak, while expanding Social Security, food stamps, and college aid.*

2. Every social problem has a governmental solution. By frustrating action, divided government impedes progress and abets public discontent. If this were so, we could create utopia. But it isn't. Consider the economy. Business cycles occur. Government can't prevent them. The effort to do so in the 1960s and 1970s fanned inflation and led to deep recessions. Government programs, taxes, and regulations affect—for better or worse—living standards. But the impact is gradual and imprecise. What truly breeds public discontent is the illusion that government can solve all problems. This fosters extravagant expectations and programs with unrealistic goals that inevitably fail.

Our political system can act when there's consensus. Consensus does not ensure good laws, but it helps produce laws acceptable to the public. This is vital in a country with as much ethnic, religious, regional, and economic diversity as ours. The trouble with single-party government is that it minimizes the need to create consensus and exaggerates the power of narrow interests in either party. The justification for this is that the people have voted for the party's "program." This is a fiction. Usually votes merely approve or disapprove of the country's present condition.

The case for one-party government would be stronger if either candidate were striving to forge a consensus on two critical issues: health care and budget deficits. In practice, neither is. Each promises

* *Divided We Govern* (Yale University Press, 1991).

painless health care reform. In reality, any effective reform would involve changes—higher spending, more government control, or less insurance coverage—that might upset many Americans. And both Clinton and Bush ignore the budget deficits. It's wishful thinking to believe that the Democrats, once in power, would suddenly attack deficits ruthlessly. Indeed, Clinton has been eagerly reassuring groups (the elderly, veterans, college students) that he can best protect their benefits.

Unlike Broder, I offer no voting booth advice. The best result for the country might be a Clinton residency and a Republican Congress. One problem today is that both parties have been entrenched too long where they are. They have become stale and smug. Reversing roles might jolt everyone and foster consensus. But my ideal outcome may be implausible, and the second-best result would be a narrow Bush victory coupled with smaller Democratic majorities. That, too, might scare people into change.

The obsession with gridlock obscures the basic problem: a genuine paralysis of the public opinion. Americans want more from government than it can deliver at today's tax levels. Both parties are equally timid in dealing with this dilemma, and, as a result, neither deserves full power.

Newsweek
September 14, 1992

THE ATTACK CULTURE

"Scandal" is the latest word to lose its meaning. The threshold for scandal has moved so low that Washington is almost never without one. The newest is the "campaign finance" scandal, but we are still dealing with the Whitewater scandal and the Gingrich scandal. We have a permanent apparatus of investigators, partisans, and reporters working full-time to discover and publicize alleged wrong-doing—and calling everything they examine a scandal or potential scandal. Growing outrage is expressed over offenses that seem ever more obscure or trivial.

Of course, there are genuine scandals, and the behavior of our highest (or lowest) officials must be open to scrutiny. Government and the people who run it can be accountable only if their activities can be inspected. But the process has become twisted into a parody. At last week's press conference, President Clinton was asked 18 questions; 15 concerned campaign fund-raising. Was that the only important matter?

What we're seeing is the attack culture. By attack culture, I mean a mind-set and set of practices that go beyond ordinary partisanship, criticism, debate, and investigation. What defines the attack culture is that its animating spirit—unexpressed but obvious—is to destroy and bring down. Does anyone doubt that the assorted Whitewater investigations aim to destroy President Clinton and the First Lady? Does anyone doubt that the charges against House Speaker Gingrich were motivated less by ethical sensitivities than the desire to annihilate him politically?

Investigation, always a political weapon, is now more so than ever. In a 1990 book (*Politics by Other Means*), political scientists Benjamin Ginsberg and Martin Shefter correctly observed: "American politics has recently undergone a fundamental transformation. . . . [C]ontending forces are increasingly relying on such institutional weapons of political struggle as legislative investigations, media revelations, and judicial proceedings to weaken their political rivals and gain power for themselves."

The attack culture originated with Watergate, and Nixon—destroyed and forced to resign—remains the standard of success. The mimicking of Watergate is increasingly undemocratic and breeds disrespect for the law, politics, and (if anyone cares) the press. Most Americans sense that the process is out of control, because no one— no one, that is, who doesn't study these scandals for countless hours—can understand what they're about.

What was Gingrich's great offense? Well, he taught a college course (a sin?). Then, some videotapes of the course were used for political promotion (gee, a politician acting political). But wait: The course was financed by tax-deductible charitable donations, which aren't allowed for politics. Therefore Gingrich committed a no-no and compounded it by providing false information to Congress (an innocent mistake, he claims; a willful deception, say his foes). Clinton may be guilty of a crime in Whitewater, but three investigations—costing more than $24 million—have yet to disclose what it is.

I am no fan of Clinton's or Gingrich's; nor am I defending their behavior and certainly wouldn't offer it as a model to my children. But we have elections for voters to decide whether, all things considered, they want to retain their elected leaders. Except in rare cases, that job shouldn't be hijacked by courts, prosecutors, or the press with investigations that are increasingly inquisitional. They aim to prejudice people against their target, even if no serious charges are ultimately sustained. The process is abused because the investigations are selective (often triggered by the target's prominence) and aim (by adverse publicity) to convict and punish the target.

The attack culture subsists on personal ambition and various political agendas. Reporters want a big story; prosecutors seek convictions; partisans crave power. And the mere act of investigation creates pressures for results. Resources have been committed; reputations are at stake. Hardly anyone wants to say, "Sorry, nothing here," or, "It's trivial." Every mistake, error, or personal excess is elevated to a great evil. Sinister motives are alleged or implied. If it's not a scandal, why bother?

It's also guilty until proven innocent. Some investigations are self-fulfilling. There are so many laws and regulations that anyone who is investigated exhaustively may be found to have violated something. And some targets, flustered or embarrassed, blunder into criminal cover-ups. Nor are the targets only prominent officials. The federal Office of Research Integrity recently cleared an experienced scientist of misconduct. But for three years he was subject to congressional hearings and had his research branded fraudulent. Those years, he said, "have been holy hell. They took away my position, my reputation, my work."

People are smeared because the attack culture is heavy-handed and single-minded. The current furor over campaign financing fits the pattern. It is driven by a coalition of Clinton haters, campaign finance reformers, and the press. The story surely seems compelling: the president (apparently) brokering the Lincoln bedroom for contributions; a host of seedy characters schmoozing at the White House; Al Gore dialing for dollars from his office.

What's missing is perspective. The $2.96 million returned by the Democratic National Committee constitutes only 1.3 percent of all DNC contributions. Questionable gifts didn't affect the election's outcome, and there's no evidence that donations changed any major policy. Much fund-raising is sleazy. But no one should forget that giving money to a candidate or party is a form of political speech. Donations can't easily be limited without compromising free speech. The present hysteria—nurtured by self-proclaimed reformers—intentionally obscures this point.

All the crusading doesn't reassure the public. Just the opposite. Because most people grasp that the process has been corrupted—being moved by ambition and politics—they put the attackers and the accused increasingly on the same moral plane. A plague on everyone. We become desensitized to genuine scandal because the artificial variety is so common. All democracies need to examine their officials; an enduring dilemma is how to prevent legitimate inquiry from sliding into sanctioned tyranny. When everything's a scandal, we're losing the proper balance.

The Washington Post
March 12, 1997

THE CULTIVATION OF CONFLICT

The most affecting and instructive political event of 1996 for me was a funeral I did not attend. I read about it later, and it said something important about how our political system has changed for the worse. It has lost much of its power to conciliate. Instead it often inflames conflicts that, though real, ought to be manageable. What crystallized the change for me was the funeral of David Ifshin, a lawyer who had served as counsel to President Clinton's 1992 campaign. One of the men who eulogized Ifshin was Republican Senator John McCain of Arizona.

What made this moving was not the difference of political parties. It was history. In 1970, Ifshin—then in his twenties—had visited Hanoi as an antiwar protester, while McCain—a downed navy pilot—was being held and tortured in a Vietnamese prison. That these two men had reconciled and developed respect and friendship seemed completely at odds with today's hateful political climate. It is a climate in which people increasingly view their opponents as their enemies.

The reconciliation was not a deathbed event. It had preceded by some years Ifshin's discovery of a fatal cancer. McCain had once harshly criticized Ifshin in a speech and later decided that it was a cheap shot that he regretted. Ifshin had decided that going to Hanoi—whatever his view of the war—was an unpatriotic act that dishonored American servicemen. A measure of the two men is that, in their separate tellings of their friendship, it's unclear who apologized first. (The full story is recounted by Michael Lewis in the May 13 *New Republic*.)

If Ifshin and McCain could bury their large disagreements, why are smaller differences so poisonous today? After all, theirs was no ordinary dispute. Ifshin believed the war was wrong; McCain thought it was his duty to serve. The Vietnamese held McCain for five and a half years; Ifshin's speeches were repeatedly piped into his prison. The two of them (it seemed to me) were entitled to their grudges. The conflicts of the 1960s involved life-and-death matters—or nearly so. Vietnam. Civil rights.

What's harder to understand is the present ugliness. By and large, the issues that preoccupy politics and public discourse now are less momentous and involve fewer moral absolutes than those of the 1960s. Abortion is an obvious exception. But in general, we face questions—budget deficits, affirmative action, welfare reform, economic insecurities, Medicare policies, the excesses of popular culture—that defy simple solutions and involve many ambiguities. These are issues where opponents can often learn from each other, even if they continue to disagree. Yet politics today is often routinely and gratuitously nasty.

We now have clichés to describe the prevailing spirit. Debates lack "civility," we say. Politics has become "polarized," and opponents regularly "demonize" each other. One explanation for the change, I think, lies in a crucial difference between the politics of the 1960s and the politics of the 1990s. Conflicts then bubbled up from the depths of society, and the political superstructure—the president, Congress, other elected and appointed officials—tried to grapple with them. By contrast, today's conflicts are often consciously nurtured (if not created) by political leaders and elites.

There has been a role reversal. The political leaders of the 1960s strove to resolve conflicts that they usually hadn't predicted and often didn't understand. The governing class, Democrats and Republicans alike, had to deal with mass marches, street protests, and a frontal assault—coming mostly from campuses—on the very legitimacy of the political system and almost all authority figures. The political system, often grudgingly, strove to acknowledge these pressures and channel them into formal politics. The effort was to mediate differences.

The governing class of today focuses more on merchandising differences. Your virtues are defined by your adversary's vices. It's a way of creating a political identity. If the differences are minimized or fade away, what remains? It's not just elected politicians who embrace this salesmanship. It's how advocacy groups and lobbies appeal to their members. It's how journalists and talking heads engineer their own celebrity. Debate proceeds in the superlative. The other side's argument isn't just wrong. It's ruinous. It threatens the future of (take your pick) the economy, the environment, democracy, or American society itself.

I am not arguing that we should submerge genuine differences. Healthy debate should be pointed and, at times, scathing. But I am suggesting that the cultivation of conflict—rather than its resolution—has become a larger concern of politics and that a lot of the resulting ill will is powered by self-promotion. It's hucksterism. The causes of this change aren't obvious, at least to me. Television (which encourages sensational sound bites), the growth of government (which spawns advocacy groups), and the collapse of old-time political machines (which makes politicians more insecure): all these are possibilities.

But whatever the causes, the phenomenon stretches across the political spectrum and poses clear dangers. It has already increased Americans' normal distaste for politics. Character assassination often substitutes for measured debate; that doesn't inspire respect. And the exaggerated differences among political elites—politicians, pundits, advocates—may amplify actual differences among ordinary people. In general, Americans are less splintered than they're portrayed. But we routinely witness harsh disagreements among "opinion leaders"; and we're constantly told how divided and different we are. Sooner or later we may come to think and act that way. We may forget common values.

Politics is inevitably about disagreements, and many of these matter deeply. But beyond the conflicts lie larger areas of agreement that define us as a nation and people. Among these are a tolerance of our differences. As it happens, I met both Ifshin and McCain on separate occasions, each for about 15 seconds. I cannot claim to understand precisely what motivated their reconciliation. But I suspect it was a common decency and an instinctive recognition of the importance of these larger areas of agreement. If so, their message is worth pondering for 1997.

The Washington Post
January 1, 1997

THE PRICE OF POLITICS

In politics, money is not the root of all evil, though many people think it is. In our era of casual cynicism, it's somehow comforting to think that Congress submits to those who make the biggest campaign contributions. A recent *New York Times* poll found that 79 percent of the respondents believe "government is run by a few big interests." Ross Perot clamors for campaign finance "reform," as does President Clinton.

The crusade for campaign "reform" captures a defining delusion of our time. It is that our democracy is besieged by some sinister cabal whose destruction would restore confidence in government. The nature of the cabal is constantly shifting. Sometimes it's "big interests" and "big money." At other times it's "career politicians" or arrogant "elites." But someone is messing with the system and must be obliterated. Campaign financing "reform," term limits, and a constitutional amendment mandating a balanced budget are among the favored strategies to eradicate offending cabals.

Our infatuation with these imagined cabals obscures the real and less sensational reason that our politics are so inconclusive and frustrating. It is, simply, that the questions that now dominate politics are ones on which Americans deeply disagree and, indeed, on which many individuals hold confused feelings. The conflicts over budget deficits, affirmative action, abortion, and government regulation (to name a few issues) are genuine and difficult. To inveigh against our various cabals, including the alleged evil of money, exempts us from responsibility for our political impasses. Some large and distant force is to blame.

It is true that politicians' pursuit of campaign money is often sleazy. And campaigns do cost more than ever. In a new study, political scientists Herbert E. Alexander of the University of Southern California and Anthony Corrado of Colby College estimate that the 1992 campaign cost $3.2 billion. That's nearly triple the amount in 1980, $1.2 billion. (The figures cover all campaigns, but most spending involves national offices. In 1992, presidential candidates spent about $550 million and congressional candidates another $678 million. Political parties and organizations spent almost $1 billion on national races. The rest went for state and local races.)

But these raw dollar figures are less impressive than they seem. Although campaign spending is growing, so is almost everything else. Between 1980 and 1992, the U.S. gross domestic product more than doubled (unadjusted for inflation). More important, campaign

Election Spending

*The cost of political campaigns is a trivial share of
national income—the gross domestic product (GDP).*

YEAR	CAMPAIGN COST	AS PERCENT OF GDP
1968	$300 million	.03%
1972	425 million	.04%
1976	540 million	.03%
1980	1.2 billion	.04%
1984	1.8 billion	.05%
1988	2.7 billion	.06%
1992	3.2 billion	.05%

Sources: "Financing the 1992 Election," Alexander and Corrado,
Commerce Department.

spending is tiny: *five or six one-hundredths of 1 percent of GDP* (see table). This is up from three one-hundredths of 1 percent in the 1960s. It hardly seems a high price for democracy.

Of course, it might be if campaign contributions were thoroughly corrupting. But they aren't. It is not that campaign money has never influenced the granting of a tax break, regulatory privilege, or dubious subsidy. To take one example: Archer Daniels Midland Co. and its chairman, Dwayne Andreas, are large contributors, and the company benefits from various farm programs, including subsidies for the conversion of grain into gasohol. Do campaign contributions help protect the subsidies? Probably. Did the contributions cause the subsidies? No. They exist because they enjoy strong support among farmers.

In short, campaign contributions matter a lot less than most people assume. The more important an issue, the less campaign money matters. Social Security, Medicare, and other programs for the elderly constitute more than a third of all federal spending. They have regularly expanded not because their supporters make big campaign gifts, but because these programs have huge constituencies and are highly popular. The military-industrial complex is supposedly a powerhouse of political influence. Yet after the cold war, dozens of defense contracts were canceled.

Among the skeptics who doubt that money rules politics is political scientist Alexander, perhaps the preeminent authority on campaign spending. Constituents' interests, political beliefs, and party loyalties are the main influences on Congress, he says. As Alexander notes, much campaign money goes to people who already hold strong views. Moreover, the influence of any individual "special interest" is diluted, because many special interests contribute. Bankers know that it's not easy to buy liberalized regulations, because brokers, their adversaries, give too.

Alexander opposes campaign "reform" spending limits as unworkable and undemocratic. In theory, limits now apply to presidential campaigns, but they are evaded. In 1992, Alexander and Corrado estimate, spending for George Bush exceeded the limit by

87 percent, spending for Bill Clinton by 99 percent. In an era of mass communication, spending limits impair free speech. Someone has to pay for TV time and advertising. Political speech is not a pristine dialogue; it is a chaotic struggle for public opinion. The necessity of money would be troubling if it settled elections—if candidates could buy victory. They can't. In 1994, eight of the 20 House candidates with the largest contributions lost.

The idea that campaign money fundamentally corrupts politics persists only because it is endlessly repeated by groups like Common Cause, mindlessly echoed by journalists, and proclaimed by politicians themselves. This last act is highly cynical. Politicians pander to the public's antipolitical mood by bewailing the corruption of politics and then innocently wonder why the public thinks ill of them. But the true damage of our cabal theory of politics is self-deception. Exaggerating the evil of campaign money diverts us from wrestling with the important issues that divide the nation.

Newsweek
August 28, 1995

THE STEALTH POWER BROKERS

The most revealing thing about political scientist Jeffrey Berry's recent book (*The New Liberalism: The Rising Power of Citizen Groups*) is that hardly anyone noticed it, even though its conclusion starkly contradicts conventional wisdom. After much research, Berry rejects the common view that liberalism died in the 1980s, suffocated by Ronald Reagan, wealthy business lobbies, and conservative political groups. Judged by congressional legislation and press coverage, precisely the opposite is true. Liberal lobbies in Washington have flourished. They rival business lobbies in power and crush conservative groups, such as the now defunct Moral Majority.

Since the 1960s, Berry says, liberalism's focus has changed from economic issues—redistributing income—to what he calls "post-material lifestyle concerns": environmentalism, rights of all sorts, consumer protection, and clean government. This liberalism expresses itself mainly through citizen lobbies, such as the Environmental Defense Fund, Ralph Nader's Public Citizen, and the National Organization for Women. It is these lobbies that wield power in influencing Washington's agenda and shaping its news.

Based on 30 years in Washington, this analysis instantly struck me as accurate. But with some exceptions (an excerpt in *The Washington Post*'s weekend section, several NPR interviews), the study has been ignored. Why? The answer is not that Berry is a right-wing zealot bent on exposing stealth liberalism. He's a Democrat ("I was raised as a Hubert Humphrey liberal") who has taught at Tufts University since 1974 and aims simply to plot interest group power.

To do this, he investigated major congressional proposals in 1963, 1979, and 1991. What changed? Which issues got on the agenda? Whose views made it into the press? If Congress passed legislation, who won? By Berry's count, Congress considered—foreign policy, except for trade, was excluded—205 major issues in these years. (A proposal was rated important if it generated congressional hearings and some press coverage.) Here's what he found:

• *Between 1963 and 1991, Congress's agenda moved to postmaterial issues.* In 1963, about two-thirds of proposals were economic, typified by manpower training or farm price supports. By 1991, roughly 70 percent involved postmaterial issues, such as a wetlands conservation bill and the Family Medical and Leave Act.

• *Liberal lobbies now receive highly favorable press coverage.* In the printed press (Berry used *The New York Times, The Wall Street Journal,* and the *Congressional Quarterly Weekly Report*), liberal groups represented almost half the quotes from lobbyists. Industry trade associations were about 30 percent, corporations 1 percent. Network TV news has a similar pattern.

• *Liberal lobbies increasingly win.* In 1963, business lobbies won three victories for every defeat to liberal lobbies. By 1991, business won three victories for every two defeats. Even this overstates business power, because often industry was simply repelling hostile legislation. Conservative groups, such as the Christian Coalition, had little effect on legislation.

Berry's study rebuts the notion that moneyed interests or conservative ideologues dominate Washington. The popular perception is different in part because the Republican capture of Congress in

1994 created a false impression of conservative triumph. To see whether it did, Berry examined 12 environmental issues in the 104th Congress (1995–96). He judged that environmentalists won 10. Conservatives' power is also exaggerated because some of their ideas have prevailed and are no longer conservative. On economic policy, balanced budgets—in times of plenty—and low inflation now command wide support. So, too, with welfare reform.

But the central cause of misinformation—why Berry's study went unnoticed—is that people have a stake in it. Certainly liberal lobbies do. They relish their image of impoverished groups fighting long odds against rich business lobbies. In fact, Berry finds that liberal lobbies are often well financed and highly professional. By contrast, conservative lobbies (but not business groups) are often poorly financed and poorly run. They have no interest in advertising their weakness.

The press, of course, should present a true picture—but doesn't. If it did, it would have to admit that it often aids liberal lobbies. This is the result less of a conscious effort to advance an agenda than of shared beliefs. Journalists see the story in the same way as liberal lobbyists. Business is regarded as greedy, self-interested, and undemocratic. Conservative groups are "out of touch" or socially dangerous. By contrast, liberal lobbies are public-spirited "watchdogs."

The convergence of values is easily inferred from opinion surveys. Consider a 1995 poll of Washington reporters. Only 2 percent rated themselves conservative, while 89 percent had voted for Clinton in 1992 (against 43 percent of the popular vote). Only 4 percent were Republicans (50 percent were Democrats, 37 percent independents). People with these values instinctively minimize the power of the "good guys" and make the "bad guys" look threatening. A lead story in *The New York Times,* for example, indicated that business dominated Congress's last session (CONGRESS LEAVES BUSINESS LOBBIES ALMOST ALL SMILES). Actually, the story showed that business groups won a few modest victories and played defense on minimum wage and "patient rights."

In a democracy, the vigor of liberal lobbies is healthy. They often succeed because they purport to speak for public opinion. Four-fifths of Americans, for example, see themselves as environmentalists, reports a Pew Research poll. What's unhealthy are the false stereotypes that distort who has influence. These discriminate against some views and popularize the idea that the political system—captured by undemocratic forces—is corrupt and unresponsive. In truth, politics often stalemates because public opinion stalemates. In that same Pew poll, almost half of Americans think that government regulation does more harm than good. Our present stereotypes wrongly convert legitimate disagreement into a cynical conspiracy against the public.

Newsweek
December 13, 1999

1994

Despite the hype, the historic significance of the recent Republican landslide is still being underestimated. It marks more than a shift in congressional power or the final collapse of the New Deal coalition. Its ultimate significance is psychological: it alters the way we think and talk about politics. Since the 1930s, America has seen itself as a Democratic nation, driven mainly by Democratic voters and ideas. In an instant, these presumptions have been shattered. The terms of political debate have fundamentally and, in my view, irreversibly changed.

By this, I do not mean that we are a Republican nation. It remains to be seen whether Republicans can build voter loyalty or whether Americans become political nomads, wandering aimlessly between parties and candidates. Nor will the federal government instantly shrivel. As I have written before, Big Government is here to stay, and there is no Republican plan to dismantle it. For example, the 1993 budget plan of GOP House leaders would have cut spending a bit more than $400 billion over five years—only 5 percent of the $8 trillion of spending in the same period. But none of this reduces the

Republican triumph to a random gesture inspired by voter cynicism or revulsion with Bill Clinton.

Since 1980, voters have consistently supported presidential candidates who have favored smaller government. This describes not only Ronald Reagan and George Bush, but also "new Democrat" Clinton and Ross Perot. Political "gridlock" existed mainly because voters also returned Democratic Congresses, except for a brief period (1981–86) of Republican control of the Senate. And congressional Democrats embodied a different political ethic: that of the New Deal and Great Society. It is an attitude as much as a set of ideas. It holds that energetic government should mobilize against a vast array of societal problems.

While Democrats controlled Congress, they could maintain that governmental activism reflected the views of most people. By and large, I think this claim was accepted by most Republicans, the public, and the political press corps. It is in this sense that America considered itself a "Democratic nation" despite much conflicting evidence: repeated Republican presidential wins (seven of twelve since World War II and five of seven since 1968) and a weakening of party allegiances. For example, only 13 percent of voters in 1952 split their tickets between presidential and House candidates; by 1972, ticket splitters were 30 percent of voters, and they never again went below 25 percent.

But psychologically, Democratic control of Congress neutralized these trends. In our system, power derives from "the people," and Congress is closest to the people. As a result, congressional elections infuse the victors with a great sense of superiority while imposing an equal sense of inferiority on the vanquished. Until now, modern Democrats have never seen themselves as the minority party. Republican presidential victories could be dismissed as "horse races": if the horses were different, the outcomes might have changed. Similarly, the growth of "independents" could be minimized because enough independents voted Democratic to maintain party control of Congress.

The upheaval of 1994 is to obliterate these habits of thinking. Political scientists will long argue over why Democrats ruled Congress for so long. Perhaps the country was Democratic. Perhaps Republicans fielded poor candidates. Perhaps voters preferred incumbents to protect their districts. Or perhaps shrewd redistricting worked. Whatever the causes, they are no more. Instead, the full mythical force of congressional elections has broken Democratic claims to majority status, though the majority label has not shifted to Republicans because, well, one election is just one election.

But by smashing the Democrats' claim, the election "changed the conversation," as Terry Eastland, an ex–Reagan administration official, has said. While Democrats were the majority, their ideas instantly enjoyed "mainstream" status. The landslide ended this, and the consequences are still underappreciated. To take one example: welfare reform. A few months ago, the proposal of some Republicans that unwed teenage mothers be denied welfare was thought reactionary; now it can't be so casually dismissed. The point goes beyond the merits or demerits of this proposal. It goes rather to the broader process by which congressional elections confer or revoke intangible political legitimacy.

The political conversation is shifting away from the New Deal ethic and toward an ethic of what might be called a "responsible society." Republicans (and some Democrats) pose new questions about government's competence and responsibilities. They advocate a changed division of labor among the federal, state, and local governments and, more important, between government and "the people." Activist proposals will no longer automatically be seen as respectable; cutbacks will no longer automatically be seen as irresponsible or stigmatized as "fringe" ideas.

Of course, the rhetoric here is far ahead of practical proposals. Americans may deplore Big Government, but they depend heavily on it. Specifically, most Republicans haven't yet faced this central fact: About a third of federal spending goes to older Americans through Social Security, Medicare, and other popular "entitlements."

As the baby boom ages, either these programs will be cut or spending (and taxes or deficits) will rise. Future government may do less, but it probably won't get smaller. And there are other contradictions, too. While denouncing government, some conservatives hope to use its power to promote their own causes (for example, prayer in schools).

What all this suggests is that politics will continue to be messy, full of inconsistencies, and often inconclusive. At times it won't look much different from how it has in the past. It may seem that nothing has changed. But to think that would be a huge mistake. The election did not just replace the "ins" with the "outs." It has altered the tone and direction of politics. It designated a new "mainstream" and altered politics' zone of respectability. It is not yet a new "realignment" of parties and ideas; but it is a decisive "dealignment" of the old.

The Washington Post
November 30, 1994

THEY CALL THIS A REVOLUTION?

"Revolution" is, along with "crisis," one of our most overused and misused words. We have gazillions of "crises" (the economic crisis, the environmental crisis, the drug crisis, the crime crisis, the education crisis) and almost as many "revolutions" (the computer revolution, the communications revolution, the biotechnology revolution, etc.). And now, of course, we have the "Republican revolution"—a term coined by the Republicans themselves and happily seconded by the press and most political commentators. Well, I dissent.

I do not dispute that we have had an extraordinary political upheaval. If a balanced budget ultimately passes (chances are good), the current Congress will justifiably rank as one of the most important since World War II. It is proposing huge changes with potentially far-reaching consequences. Federal-state relations may be refashioned, with states assuming more responsibility for some major programs (Medicaid, welfare). Spending for the elderly will have been dragged, uneasily, onto the political agenda. Indeed, the terms of political debate may shift decisively, if budget balancing is restored as a legitimate—and practical—discipline.

But none of this, in my view, qualifies as a revolution. What I mean by revolution is an event or trend that completely alters some system (political, social, economic) or set of ideas. Television gave us a genuine revolution in mass communications. The car constituted a genuine revolution in transportation, displacing the horse and the railroad. Each of these revolutions triggered massive social and economic side effects, many of which are still occurring and some of which are still controversial. The car, for example, transformed the nation's landscape by making suburbanization possible. And we still argue about whether TV promotes violence.

In politics, revolutions tend to be violent and to replace one regime with another. But they need not be violent. In the United States, the adoption of the Constitution was a revolution almost as important as the American Revolution itself, because the Constitution determined—a determination later challenged by the Civil War—that we would have a truly national government and not simply be a loose collection of states. The creation of the European Community (now the European Union) after World War II was another revolution. Although it did not suppress all Europe's ancient feuds, it channeled most into a peaceful framework.

Against this background, the Republican revolution doesn't look like the real McCoy. And why should it? In America, political change is usually evolutionary. It proceeds gradually, which is what most Americans want. The political changes now under way are mostly of this type. The fact that Medicare (a once off-limits program for the elderly) is being debated signals an important shift in the political climate. But the government isn't abdicating all responsibility for the elderly. Indeed, spending on them will rise—no matter whose budget is adopted—in both absolute amounts and amounts per individual.

The same can be said of programs for the poor. Most changes are at the margin. Medicaid and welfare are now jointly run by the federal government and the states. They will continue to be jointly run and financed, but the states will get more power and, compared with present programs, less money. The point is not whether these changes will make the poor more self-sufficient (as advocates argue) or whether they will further impoverish the poor (as critics claim). It is simply that the changes are not revolutionary. The basic principle (government has a responsibility for the poor) remains, while details change.

The contrived "Republican revolution" is mostly a political and journalistic convenience. Many new Republican members of Congress wanted to distance themselves as far as possible from Washington's ruling elites and, thus, found "revolutionary" a useful and flattering label. It conveyed the sense that they were true outsiders, who had no desire to perpetuate the status quo in the capital. They would tear it down. The press eagerly endorsed this self-styled revolution, because it made an already dramatic political story even more so.

By now, shrewder Republicans must regret their word selection. It is a public relations disaster and a political gift to the Democrats. Though unhappy with politics as usual, Americans aren't revolutionaries. Indeed, the idea of "revolution" gives most Americans the creeps. The term evokes the specter of disorder and anarchy. Naturally, Democrats have preyed on these associations and anxieties. Republicans have been called "extremists" and "terrorists" who would scorch the social safety net and jeopardize Americans' sense of security. That would be revolutionary, but it isn't what the Republicans propose.

Does any of this matter? It's only a word, after all. Perhaps the careless use of language doesn't make a difference in many contexts. We may or may not be undergoing a "computer revolution." What you call it is a matter of taste and judgment. History will ultimately decide. But in politics, words do matter. They help create a climate of opinion. The abuse of language subverts reasoned debate. Exaggeration, simplification, and distortion are normal parts of political debate. But the more these excesses are compounded, the harder discussion becomes.

In a partisan sense, the Republicans deserve what they get. They decided to call themselves revolutionaries; now they suffer the consequences. But the press also bears some responsibility for having popularized the idea, and in a larger sense, the country is the ultimate loser for this misrepresentation. All change is not revolutionary. When we mischaracterize—and stigmatize—it as such, we let symbolism overwhelm substance. People are frightened from making any change, because it seems larger and more disruptive than it actually is. The irony is that we then make it more difficult to create a consensus for the evolutionary change that most Americans actually desire.

The Washington Post
January 3, 1996

WASHINGTON DISCONNECTED

Thirty years ago [in 1969], I came to Washington as a reporter of 23. Since then I have never witnessed such a huge disconnect as now between the nation's capital and the rest of the country. The capital is transfixed by Clinton's impeachment. Meanwhile the rest of the country hardly seems to care. Most Americans felt that 1998 was a good year for them (72 percent) and their community (78 percent), reports a poll by the Pew Research Center. Impeachment? Only 32 percent had followed the story closely; and 64 percent said that "the media is giving [it] too much attention."

It's arguable that this distance is an isolated event, reflecting the peculiarity of the Clinton presidency and the carefree attitudes of a booming economy. This is, I think, a delusion. These conditions may have enlarged the disconnect, but the growing separation of Washington from the rest of the country is no fluke. It's one of the defining trends of my three decades here. Over this period, Washington has grown more insular. People elsewhere tune out because they feel left out.

By Washington, I do not mean the place. Believe it or not, most people here lead lives like most other Americans'. They endure congestion, worry about schools, and think only intermittently about politics and government. Indeed, this Washington depends less than ever on government. Since 1970, the metropolitan area's population has grown roughly 60 percent to 4.6 million. This growth stems heavily from industries that could locate almost anywhere. America Online operates from a suburb; *Newsweek* picked the area as one of its ten high-tech centers.

What I mean by Washington is the political community—the "inside the Beltway" crowd or "governing class." It consists of politicians, congressional staffers, White House aides, political appointees, top bureaucrats, the press, lobbyists, think-tank experts, and the staffs of interest and advocacy groups. These folks subsist on politics, elections, legislation, and public policy.

The widening gap between this Washington and the rest of the country is not altogether bad. America thrives in part because it's decentralized. Governmental power remains dispersed among the national, state, and local levels. The economy permits companies to expand, compete, contract, and expire largely on their own. There is plenty of volunteerism, charity, and philanthropy. The *Statistical Abstract,* for example, counts 330,000 churches and 40,000 foundations.

America can do well without Washington's doing well. In a recent *New Republic,* Gregg Easterbrook noted some signs of ongoing national improvement: In 1997, the homicide rate was the lowest in 30 years; a typical new home is 40 percent larger than in 1970; births to teen mothers have dropped 12 percent since 1991; smog is down a third since 1970. Some gains—say, environmental improvement—stem from Washington; most do not.

Still, there's something intuitively disturbing about Washington's growing disconnect. In a representative democracy, people shouldn't feel less and less represented. The war in Vietnam and Watergate are routinely advanced to explain the deep mistrust of politicians and government. But their impact is overstated. Almost a third of American adults were under ten or not even born when Nixon left office in 1974.

When I arrived in Washington in 1969, it was widely believed that government could solve most social problems. This faith—plus confidence that the economy could produce boundless new wealth—inspired immense governmental activism. Washington connected with the rest of the country by showering new benefits on many constituencies. Although Democrats led this crusade, most Republicans (including, prominently, Nixon) joined. The elderly benefited from Medicare and higher Social Security; the poor received Medicaid and food stamps; schools and universities got more aid; Congress passed environmental and worker safety laws.

We know now that this crusade foundered on its own heady assumptions. All social problems could not be solved; the economy couldn't produce boundless wealth; budget deficits emerged because politicians wouldn't choose between higher taxes and lower spending; regulations involved costs as well as benefits. The political impact of this failure was profound. Lost was the old formula for connecting with the mass of moderate voters. Ever since, both parties have struggled vainly to find a new one. I am simplifying only slightly when I say that the result is two parties that—at least in rhetoric—are not so much liberal and conservative as reactionary and radical.

Democrats are reactionary because they seem to promise a return to the dreamy 1960s with expanding social programs and constituent benefits. Many Americans are suspicious. On the other hand, Republicans seem radical because, blaming government for almost any problem, they seem too ready to dismantle it. This frightens most Americans, who (despite misgivings) like their government benefits, from college loans to Social Security. Neither party commands the critical center; both offend it.

It is in this broader sense that Washington has become disconnected. The parties can't speak convincingly to the messy reality of large but inevitably limited government. Political rhetoric often seems contrived. Except in token ways, Democrats can't create new programs and Republicans can't cut taxes. Barred from genuine action, politicians become more strident in their debates and more vicious in their personal attacks. They consort mostly with their own "core constituencies" and sympathetic ideologues, deepening their isolation and illusions.

This insularity exposes Washington types, of all political stripes, to shocks from the hinterlands. Democrats were stunned by their loss of Congress in 1994; Republicans were stunned by their setbacks in 1998. Americans have increasingly defined down what they expect of political leaders. In Washington, Clinton's impeachment seems extraordinary; elsewhere, it's seen as the same old stuff, albeit at a higher level. This is a sad and apt commentary on three decades of change: Washington, though no less interesting, has lost touch and respect.

Newsweek
January 11, 1999

FREEDOM FROM POLITICS

We pundits constantly concoct new trends that ignore history and common sense. Our latest invention is the idea that Americans have grown more selfish and indifferent to national life than ever. Commentators on the right are appalled that the public isn't so outraged by President Clinton's behavior as to want him impeached. Commentators on the left decry a public so self-centered that it won't support vast new social programs. The shared belief is that self-absorbed Americans are smothering democracy. Golly, voter turnout in the last congressional election, at 36 percent, was the lowest since 1942.

Do modern Americans deserve this scorn? Not really.

Consider a new survey of 800 parents by the nonpartisan Public Agenda Foundation. The poll asked if the United States is a "unique country that stands for something special" or "just another country whose system is no better or worse" than others. The response: 84 percent rated the United States unique. There's nothing new here. Polls regularly show that we feel better about our country than citizens elsewhere feel about theirs. One Gallup poll in the early 1990s

asked people in 15 countries whether they would like to move elsewhere. Americans were second from the bottom. About 11 percent
said they would move, compared with 30 percent of Germans and
21 percent of the French.

Americans care deeply about their country, and the freedom from
politics—especially in periods lacking a national crisis—is one of
the things they like best. In the Public Agenda survey, 61 percent of
the respondents said that what they most value about America are its
"personal freedoms." By contrast, only 13 percent cited "political
freedoms." There's nothing new here, either. In a study in the 1950s,
political scientist Robert Dahl of Yale found, not surprisingly, that
"food, sex, love, family, work, play, shelter, comfort [and] friendship"—and "not politics"—preoccupied most people.

The punditocracy can't grasp this truth. Recently in *The New
York Times Magazine,* the journalist Nicholas Lemann proclaimed
the arrival of "government of, by and for the comfortable." People
believe, he wrote, "that government has a very serious obligation to
the middle class . . . [but] the middle class is in no way obligated to
commit time or money to larger national projects." He ignored the
awkward fact that federal taxes are near historic highs, almost 21
percent of national income. Then he argued that present beliefs reject "the traditional view" that "government can assume the loyalty
and trust of its citizens as it goes about using its resources to do the
country's business."

What "tradition" is this? It's not the American tradition, with its
historic emphasis on individualism and suspicion of government. In
the 1830s, the Frenchman Alexis de Tocqueville wrote that "an
American attends to his private affairs as if he were alone in the
world." In the 1880s, most Americans felt "the less government the
better," observed James Bryce of Britain.

It's also wrong to see voter turnout as the main indicator of public spiritedness. Doubters should read a superb new book, *The Good
Citizen,* by sociologist Michael Schudson of the University of California at San Diego. True, voter turnout was much higher (often 75
to 80 percent) in the nineteenth century. But comparisons are

strained, as Schudson shows. For starters, many Americans couldn't vote. Women couldn't vote in national elections until the ratification of the 19th Amendment in 1920. Except for a brief period after the Civil War, many black Americans couldn't vote until the Voting Rights Act of 1965.

Beyond these large details, politics then wasn't what it is now. Especially after the Civil War, it also served as popular entertainment and a job bank. Political parties organized torchlight parades and sponsored glee clubs. Victorious parties rewarded supporters with government jobs. The postal service was a vast source of patronage. In 1896, it provided 78,500 jobs. Parties financed themselves by assessments on the salaries of patronage job holders (a typical rate was 3 percent). Voters sometimes were paid to vote, with either a job or an outright bribe. Debate on "the issues" was narrow.

"The more politics could be understood as team sport and the rivalry of social groups, the more enthusiastically people participated," wrote Schudson. But parties weakened with the rise of mass entertainment (vaudeville, movies, baseball) and civil service reform, which cut patronage jobs. "How are you goin' to interest our young men in the country if you have no office to give them when they work for their party?" George Washington Plunkitt, a nineteenth-century political boss, once asked.

Here lie the deeper causes of receding voter turnout. As politics has become more earnest and abstract, it has also become less engaging and less directly connected to people's personal self-interest. There are so many issues that even conscientious citizens can't stay abreast. Also, the ways to alter social policy have proliferated, as Schudson notes. People can resort to the courts, agencies, publicity, or protest.

All this has reduced the importance of elections. They can show popular disapproval of how government is performing and can even give government a general shove in a different direction. But elections are less and less a means to manipulate specific policies or, outside of crises, to sanction radical transformations. Although democracy requires oversight, this job increasingly falls—for good and ill—to interest groups and the press.

It's hard to defend low voter turnout, but it's doubtful that an increase would result in dramatic changes in government policy. Complaints of pundits about public indifference mostly reflect hurt feelings. We can't accept that most people aren't interested in what we think, say, and write. People devote their time to what they can most influence and what matters most to them (their jobs, families, and leisures); politics suffers in this competition. Who is to say they are wrong?

The Washington Post
December 2, 1998

PART III

ECONOMICS

ORIGINAL SIN REMEMBERED

We are still suffering [in June 1992] from the legacy of a commencement address given by John Kennedy 30 years ago this month at Yale. The speech was then seen as a daring statement of new economic principles, and, with hindsight, it may rank as the most important presidential pronouncement on economic policy since World War II. Unfortunately, it led us in the wrong direction: toward high inflation and runaway budget deficits.

Economic mythology, Kennedy argued, was obstructing the nation's progress. "The great enemy of truth is very often not the lie—deliberate, contrived, and dishonest—but the myth—persistent, persuasive, and unrealistic," he said. Specifically, budget deficits were not automatically bad, and the danger of inflation was vastly overstated.

But what Kennedy denounced as "myths" were actually valuable traditions and taboos: things we practiced out of habit or avoided out of fear. We had a tradition of low inflation (in 1960, it was 1.4 percent). And there was a taboo against budget deficits. President Eisenhower had railed against them (he balanced his budgets three

or four years out of eight—depending on how they're measured—
and deficits were relatively small). Once these constraints were
swept away, we became prey to foolish policies.

Kennedy's Yale speech was, in some ways, the original sin. It
ditched the prevailing orthodoxies and left the country rudderless:
committed to desirable goals without the means to reach them. With
hindsight, the sin is understandable. Kennedy had pledged to get the
country moving and was also a creature of his time: a period of high
optimism when people believed that technology and society's best
minds could guarantee social improvement. His economists were
self-confident academics who thought the stodgy Eisenhower had
depressed economic growth and raised unemployment. They knew
they could do better.

When Kennedy arrived at Yale June 11, he was under siege. The
stock market was in a tailspin. On May 28, it had dropped nearly 6
percent. In April, the president had fought the steel industry over
price increases. The White House's allegedly antibusiness bias and
high spending were being blamed for a loss of confidence. "If
Kennedy had a heart attack," *Newsweek* quoted a bitter businessman
as saying, "[stock] prices would jump 40 points." (That's equivalent
to a 230-point rise on the Dow today.)*

On June 7, Kennedy announced at a press conference that he
would seek a new tax cut to stimulate the economy. He resolved to
use the Yale speech as a way to convince opponents that more energetic policies were sensible and prudent. The speech, biographer
Arthur M. Schlesinger Jr. has written, was an appeal to "reason" intended to broach a dialogue with business leaders.

What's striking about the speech today is its calculated confusion. Everything is complex, Kennedy said. "What we need is not
labels and clichés but more basic discussion of the sophisticated and
technical questions. . . ." Economic policies, he argued, involved
"subtle challenges for which technical answers, not political answers, must be provided." The whole idea was to replace tradition

---

* In 2000, the equivalent change would have been about 700 points.

and taboo with trust in modern thinking and experts: that is, economists. (But the hold of the past was strong. Not until 1964, after
Kennedy's assassination, did Congress pass the tax cut.)

What we know now is that Kennedy's exchange—technocrats for
tradition—was doomed by two flaws. First, economists didn't know
enough to do what he expected. They couldn't create permanent
"full employment" (then defined as a 4 percent unemployment rate)
without inflation. And second, politicians could now rationalize
careless policies in the guise of enlightened economics. Deficits
were okay, because they would increase economic growth and ultimately balance the budget. Faster growth made new spending programs affordable. Low interest rates were justified to increase
growth.

More generally, Kennedy's basic premise was wrong. True,
things are complicated. But that does not obviate the need for core
beliefs—intuitively understood by the public and workable in practice—to inform and constrain government policies. Kennedy's
shortcoming, shared to a greater or lesser extent by his successors,
was an inability to find such principles and communicate them to
the public.

No one has yet improved on Eisenhower's principles, as Ray-
mond J. Saulnier, one of his chief advisers, shows in a new book.*
If people want a new government service, they have to pay for it
through taxes. Government doesn't create economic growth. People
and businesses do (though government may temporarily influence
growth). And containing inflation is essential for a healthy economy. Eisenhower was stubborn but not rigid in adherence to his
principles. He tolerated deficits in recessions, for example, but re-
sisted tax cuts or spending increases that would create a long-term
imbalance.

Without basic beliefs, we lack a framework to discipline government policies. The faith of Kennedy and his advisers in "reason"

---

* *Constructive Years: The U.S. Economy under Eisenhower* (University Press of
America, 1991).

was, to some extent, unreasonable. We cannot always know in advance that things that are bad for us will actually be bad. A little inflation wasn't so bad. But it led to more inflation, which led to more—and that *was* bad. When small, deficits seemed easily tolerable. We became accustomed to them, and that led slowly to the bigger deficits that are now paralyzing government. In 1959, interest payments were 6.3 percent of federal spending; by 1990, they were nearly 15 percent.

Bad ideas, once unleashed, linger in their consequences. We have now been practiced on by successive waves of economic sorcerers, each trying to retrieve the unrealistic promises of the 1960s. The overblown rhetoric of Republican supply-siders in the early 1980s strongly resembled that of the Kennedy-Johnson economists. We partially eradicated high inflation, but only by enduring the severe 1981–82 recession. And now we are toying with a dubious scheme to codify—through a constitutional amendment requiring a balanced budget—political norms that commanded widespread public respect in the 1950s. Such is history's revenge.

Newsweek
June 8, 1992

AGE OF VOLCKER

On history's blackboard, most public figures—the politicians and bureaucrats who dominate daily headlines—leave barely a mark. They are too powerless or purposeless to make a difference. They are mainly swept along by the sea of events, shouting loudly as they go to convince themselves and everyone else that they matter. It's a deception and a fraud. Paul Volcker was not one of these. He shaped history as well as being shaped by it.

The business of the Federal Reserve—managing interest rates, money flows, and credit availability—is so technical and remote that the true scope of Volcker's achievement may not be appreciated. No one disputes his main accomplishment: subduing the most stubborn peacetime inflation in U.S. history. But Volcker's triumph extends beyond this. He presided over the economy during the period of its greatest stress and danger since World War II, and no great calamity occurred on his watch.

No one can say what might have happened if Volcker had not been there. The grim possibilities exist only by way of analogy. The last time the U.S. economy experienced comparable uncertainty was in the late 1920s. Many economists believe that with better Federal Reserve leadership, the Great Depression might have been averted. Facing unprecedented problems, the Federal Reserve of the early 1930s couldn't cope. It permitted a banking crisis that cascaded into an economic collapse. Volcker faced equally unfamiliar problems. The absence of a crisis measures his skill.

More is involved than a feat of economic management. Mastering inflation has restored confidence in our capacity to govern. The accelerating inflation of the Carter presidency touched everyone and corroded Americans' optimism. The antidote wasn't subtle. In the 1981–82 recession, unemployment reached a peak of 12.1 million, and the factory utilization rate dropped to 69.5 percent. But Volcker's success disproved all the elaborate excuses (higher oil prices, indexed wages, etc.) of why government couldn't contain inflation. And the subsequent recovery has quieted the argument that inflation's cure would be worse than the disease.

To say this is not to say Volcker has created a state of economic bliss. Everyone knows today's problems. Agriculture remains depressed. Banks are overburdened with dubious loans to farmers, developing countries, oil drillers, and real estate developers. The U.S. trade deficit is the largest ever, and some manufacturers haven't revived from the recession and import competition. But many of these problems are the aftershocks of high inflation, and they have—so far—remained isolated. They didn't coalesce into a general economic collapse and haven't kept the recovery from entering its fifth year.

Nor, obviously, did Volcker single-handedly conduct the crusade against inflation. The alliance between Volcker and Ronald Reagan was a happy accident: neither could have done so well without the other. Although Reagan opposed inflation (who didn't?), he had no forethought of savagely stamping it out. But once Volcker started the job, the president supported him. Criticism from Congress grew. Home builders, auto dealers, and real estate agents mailed thousands of keys to Volcker as symbols of unsold houses and cars and threatened bankruptcies. But Reagan didn't wave Volcker off.

The episode underlines the ambiguous relationship between the White House and the Federal Reserve. Technically "independent," the Federal Reserve has huge latitude to run its interest rate and credit policies on a daily basis. But it cannot maintain a truly independent economic policy in defiance of the White House. What bonded Volcker and Reagan—who spoke rarely and have little personal rapport—was patience and a conviction that uncontrolled inflation endangers a productive and democratic society. Reagan's patience was richly rewarded. Inflation's decline remains his greatest accomplishment and ensured his reelection.

Volcker had become what most public figures yearn for and never attain: a legend in his time. The reputation is deserved and yet distorts reality. He had luck. The economy has its own rhythms and recuperative powers. Moreover, there was much that Volcker failed to predict: the severity of the 1981–82 recession; the sharpness of inflation's fall; the huge rise in the dollar's exchange rate between 1980 and 1985; and the extent of the international debt crisis. But if Volcker didn't control events, neither did he allow himself to be controlled by them. As an economic tactician, he had two great virtues.

First, he had a better grasp than most U.S. officials or economists of the importance of the international economy. In 1982, Volcker helped defuse the international debt crisis. Had that been left to Donald Regan's Treasury, it's hard to know what might have happened.

Second, he could see through the veil of economic statistics and theory to the real world. After the recession, neither interest rates nor money supply statistics provided an accurate guide to Federal Reserve policy. High interest rates implied credit was tight, while a rapidly expanding money supply indicated it was easy. Volcker became a slave to neither.

What emerged was an acute sense of timing. He knew when to change emphasis, as in 1982 when he shifted from suppressing inflation to promoting growth. But to call Volcker a "pragmatist" (as is often done) is wrong. All his flexibility and attention to detail were ultimately directed toward fulfilling strongly held beliefs about what's vital for preserving a democratic society and a healthy economy. Chief among these values was the importance of regaining price stability—a goal he almost attained.

His legacy is blurred, because his achievement can be so easily undone. Avoiding inflation's long-term hazards involves periodically accepting the temporary hardships of recessions. Otherwise, inflation gradually rises until it becomes so strong that it can be controlled only at a brutal social cost, or not at all. That dilemma should never recur if anything has been learned from Volcker's experience. He's been a giant among midgets, but only time will tell whether Americans have the discipline and wisdom to grasp the meaning of what he did.

Newsweek
June 15, 1987

THE TRIUMPH OF FOLK WISDOM

We are now completing [in the late 1990s] a 40-year political and intellectual journey whose termination seems symbolized by two events last week: the announcement of a bipartisan agreement to balance the budget by 2002, and the latest unemployment rate, which—at 4.9 percent—is the lowest since 1973. These events mark a passage in how we think about the economy and government. They signal the reassertion of folk wisdom over professional economics. The folk ideas that are now triumphant are the desirability of stable money (that is, low or nonexistent inflation) and of balanced budgets. We don't have either, but we do have a broad consensus that both serve the nation's long-term well-being.

As recently as the late 1950s, these ideas commanded popular thinking. They were regarded as prudent disciplines. Government shouldn't, in normal times, spend more than it taxes; balancing the budget compelled politicians to choose between the hurt of higher taxes and the benefits of higher spending. And stable money fostered stability in the economy and social relations. But in the 1960s, these durable traditions were ridiculed and discarded. Economists dismissed them as old-fashioned and harmful. A bit of inflation, they argued, could lower unemployment. Wisely used, budget deficits could avert recessions.

Because these supposedly sophisticated theories never delivered, we have now come full circle. The significance of the new budget agreement transcends its particular merits and demerits (there are both) or even its ability to reach balance by 2002. It lies mainly in the fact that the goal of a balanced budget has been embraced across much of the political spectrum. What people aim to achieve—even if they fall short—affects how they behave and what's considered legitimate and illegitimate. Only recently has a balanced budget attained such widespread support. When elected in 1992, for example, President Clinton merely supported "deficit reduction."

The pursuit of "stable money" is, in similar fashion, now a central aim of government economic policy in a way that it hadn't been. Two decades ago, the phrase had vanished from economic discussion. Economists and government officials talked instead of containing inflation to tolerable levels and reconciling it with sustained economic growth and low unemployment. By contrast, the hallmark of this economic expansion has not been the promise of the Federal Reserve to maintain it forever, but rather the routine warnings that government must prevent a resurgence of inflation.

Our views have shifted mostly as the result of bitter experience. Recall the record. In 1960, inflation was 1.4 percent. By 1979, it was 13.3 percent. The effort to "manage" the economy for greater stability and lower unemployment led instead to more instability and higher unemployment. Recessions were not avoided and, when they occurred, tended to be harsher. In 1975, unemployment averaged 8.5 percent. In 1982, it averaged 9.7 percent. In general, government policies grew more muddled and unpredictable, as many futile tactics—wage and price controls and guidelines, credit controls—were tried against inflation.

Meanwhile budget discipline was lost. It is true that budget deficits expanded under President Reagan, but the decisive events in the creation of perpetual deficits—the abandonment of the tradition that inhibited them—occurred under presidents Kennedy, Johnson, and Nixon with the aid of successive Democratic Congresses. Deficits were tolerated as enlightened when, in fact, they were merely expedient. Since 1961, the budget has been in surplus in only one year (1969).

We've come back to older traditions because, simply, the alternatives are worse. One reason a budget agreement has been possible is that the economy has been stronger than expected, leading to lower unemployment and higher tax revenues. The fact that so many economists (including many who promoted the foolish policies of the 1960s and 1970s) are so astonished merely reaffirms the superficiality of their economic understanding. Psychology matters: a lesson they've never truly grasped.

The 1960s' pledge to prevent recessions made companies and workers irresponsible. They felt they could raise prices and wages without their inflationary behavior being punished by lower profits or lost jobs. Since the early 1980s, these self-defeating assumptions have given way. The unwillingness to tolerate ever-rising inflation has meant that companies and workers could suffer if their wages or prices got out of line. Intensified competition from other sources (imports, deregulation, new technology) reinforced the lesson. Economic insecurity has increased for many individuals and firms. But, paradoxically, these market pressures have promoted overall stability. Companies restrain labor costs. Lower labor costs foster more hiring. Subdued inflation limits harsh anti-inflationary policies.

We are also reverting to the notion that the budget is mainly a framework for determining the role of government and less an instrument of economic policy. There is little talk now of the economic virtues of deficits or even of balanced budgets. Both have been hard to detect. Deficits never had their advertised benefits; but persistent deficits didn't cause instant calamity, either. (If they had, they would have been addressed sooner.) So Congress and the president—and the public—are drifting toward traditional ideas: the belief that large peacetime deficits shift the tax burden onto future generations and a commonsense faith that pleasant spending should be checked by unpleasant taxes.

The rediscovery of old virtues won't solve all our problems. Balanced budgets aren't always appropriate (wars and economic slumps are exceptions). And just because a government balances its budget does not mean it will operate wisely. It may impose unfair or oppressive taxes. It may spend too little or too much. Nor does a commitment to stable money ensure, by itself, economic utopia. It will not prevent slumps or brief spurts of inflation. Nor will it guarantee growth. Though Europe and Japan have low inflation, their growth falters for other reasons. But these folk virtues are needed for national success. Their recovery makes you wonder where we'd be now if they'd never been lost.

The Washington Post
May 7, 1997

WE'RE NOT A NATIONAL
LAUNDROMAT

One of the most misunderstood and maligned concepts around these days is the "service economy." It's frowned upon, summoning up a vision of fast-food restaurants, dry cleaners, and bowling alleys—a nation that produces nothing of enduring value. All this is the engaging stuff of cocktail party economics. It's also wrong: the intellectual equivalent of believing, in the fifteenth century, that the world was flat.

Popular preconceptions about the service economy are generally cockeyed. It is not inexorably leading to lower living standards (actually, just the opposite). It is not displacing the physical production of goods (also, the opposite). It is not polarizing income between a well-paid elite of professionals and a poorly paid proletariat of janitors. And it is not spawning a nation of Laundromats and barbershops.

Mostly, the expansion of the service sector is a sign of national wealth, not decay. As the economy has evolved, labor has moved from farming, then to goods production (manufacturing, mining, construction), and after that to services—not because production was declining, but because more production could be done with relatively fewer people. Farm production today is many times the 1860 level; yet farming requires less than 4 percent of the workforce, compared with 60 percent then.

Manufacturing has undergone the same change. In 1980, its output was one-third higher than in 1970, but employment had grown only 5 percent. More workers have been freed to provide services that a poorer society could not afford or did not want. There are more hotels, amusement parks, and professional sports teams because there is more mobility and more leisure. There are more hospitals, doctors, and nursing homes because we live longer and can spend more on our upkeep.

To think that the service economy portends misfortune is to assume that it's a new phenomenon—but it isn't. Traditionally, economists have classified production of anything that can be stored (like a car) into the goods sector and everything else into the service sector. So services include retail stores, wholesale distributors, telephone and power utilities, banks, and government. Since the late 1940s, services have accounted for half of all jobs; today, the proportion is 7 of 10. If the shift was going to cause trouble, it should have already occurred.

Anyone who thinks manufacturing is especially virtuous should also study some comparisons. North Carolina has more of its nonfarm workforce in manufacturing (32.8 percent in 1983) than any other state. But its residents' per capita income—the money available to each of them—ranks only 39th. The following table shows that North Carolina is no exception; most states with big manufacturing bases aren't near the top in income.

This doesn't mean that manufacturing fosters poverty; it simply confirms the process of historic change. Fifty years ago, North and South Carolina were largely rural, farm economies. As farms mechanized, tenant farmers and farmhands moved into factories. The pay was poor by Northern standards, but it was better than subsistence farming. Living standards in these states—their per capita incomes—are much closer to the national average now than in 1940.

Shattering a Myth

States with the highest proportion of manufacturing workers don't have the highest per capita incomes. Service jobs pay well, too.

	Percent of factory workers*	Annual per capita income and rank among the states*
N. Carolina	32.8%	$ 9,656 (39)
S. Carolina	30.6%	$ 8,954 (48)
Rhode Island	29.3%	$11,504 (23)
Indiana	28.7%	$10,567 (33)
Connecticut	27.9%	$14,826 (2)
New Hampshire	27.7%	$11,620 (19)
Michigan	27.6%	$11,574 (21)
Tennessee	27.3%	$ 9,362 (42)
Arkansas	27.0%	$ 9,040 (46)
Wisconsin	26.1%	$11,132 (27)

Sources: Bureau of Labor Statistics, Bureau of Economic Analysis.

* 1983 figures

These comparisons also emphasize the huge diversity in both the goods and service sectors. Some industries and jobs pay well; others don't. The sloppy assumption that all manufacturing workers are well-paid autoworkers and that every service worker is shoveling french fries at McDonald's obscures this reality. Although goods-producing industries do (on average) pay more than service industries, there's no solid evidence—despite claims to the contrary—that the rise of service employment has made income distribution more unequal.

Why not? Some guesses. First, average wages in the service industry are held down by the large number of women and teenagers who are in part-time jobs. Almost a quarter of working women, for example, voluntarily have part-time jobs. Most of these workers aren't their family's primary earners. In fact, these jobs provide flexibility for families in balancing home or school responsibilities with the need for income.

Second, many fast-growing service industries do pay well. Between 1975 and 1983, "business services" accounted for about one in seven new jobs. True, this category includes low-paid janitorial services, where average wages ($5.94 an hour in 1983) were below manufacturing's ($8.83). But it also includes architectural and engineering firms ($11.50), computer firms ($10.06), and accounting firms ($8.97).

The paradox of the service economy is that most of us belong to it, yet there's a bias against it. Our manufacturing mentality imputes superiority to tangible products. But almost everything people buy (food is the major exception) provides a service. Cars and planes provide transportation; houses provide shelter; television sets provide information and entertainment.

In the real world, the distinction blurs even more. Xerox is a major manufacturer, but only one-seventh of its American workforce is on the factory floor. More than half are involved in sales, customer service, and marketing. Xerox's machines wouldn't be worth much if customers didn't know about them (because there was no advertising or sales force) or couldn't use them (because there was no training or repair). So most Xerox workers provide these services.

The same applies to most industries; for example, as many people work at auto dealerships as work in auto manufacturing. The distinction between services and manufacturing is increasingly irrelevant for higher living standards and more jobs. We should encourage efficient firms over the inefficient and growth industries over the stagnant—whatever they may be. Old stereotypes are not a good way either to understand the economy or to improve it.

Newsweek
July 9, 1984

DOWNSIZING FOR GROWTH

[Many] labor market observers have asserted that the link between workers and employers has become more tenuous and short term . . . labor market statistics, however, call into question the extent of any move toward less job stability.
—Report on the American Work Force,
U.S. Department of Labor, 1995

As the Labor Department report shows, the hysteria over downsizing—whipped up in part by Labor Secretary Robert Reich and a massive series in *The New York Times*—is just that. Companies are resorting more often to layoffs, but there never was a time of absolute job security, and downsizing doesn't destroy most stable jobs. I have written about all this before, but now I want to extend the discussion and suggest that, in some respects, downsizing may improve the economy.

It seems counterintuitive. We are uneasy with the possibility that what's bad for individual workers and firms—job insecurity, bankruptcy—may be good for society. But this may be, and the argument is not simply that downsizing enables some companies to survive. The notion is broader: it is that the anxieties and uncertainties that unsettle people may make them more prudent and productive in ways that strengthen and stabilize the economy.

Though little noted, the present economic expansion recently became the third longest since World War II. It has lasted almost five years and is exceeded only by the expansions of the 1960s (106 months, from February 1961 to December 1969) and of the 1980s (92 months, from November 1982 to July 1990). But in some ways, it is superior to these because it hasn't yet spawned higher inflation. Since 1990, inflation has dropped from 6.1 to 2.5 percent. By contrast, it rose in the 1960s, from 1.4 percent in 1960 to 6.2 percent in 1969.

The 1960s boom is often viewed nostalgically as a "golden age," when it actually set the stage for the most turbulent and least productive economic period since 1945. The severity of the two worst postwar recessions (those of 1973–75 and 1981–82, with peak monthly unemployment rates of 9 and 10.8 percent, respectively) stemmed directly from double-digit inflation (12.3 percent in 1974 and 13.3 percent in 1979). And the global competitiveness of many U.S. industries eroded; between 1971 and 1980, for instance, car imports rose from 15 to 27 percent of U.S. sales.

We are much better off today in most respects. What happened? The answer, I think, is that there has been a profound shift in economic ideas, which, though improving the economy, offends Reich and the *Times*. From the 1960s to the early 1980s, government officials and corporate managers consciously strove to expand employment, eliminate recessions, and enhance job security. Keynesian economics dominated; "responsible" companies promised, implicitly or explicitly, lifetime jobs.

The experiment failed: the concerted pursuit of these worthwhile goals—total job security and economic stability—gave us higher unemployment as well as higher inflation. In the 1980s, economic ideas changed. The Federal Reserve moved ruthlessly against inflation; now the Fed worries most about attaining "price stability." Meanwhile, companies grew less concerned with saving jobs and focused more on raising market share and profits.

The result is that, since then, average unemployment has dropped, the one subsequent recession in 1990–91 was fairly mild (peak monthly unemployment was 7.8 percent), and industrial competitiveness has advanced. One reason for improvement is that we finally recognized that the promises of economic stability and job security were self-defeating; they perversely inspired behavior that made both goals harder to achieve. When people expected government to avoid economic slumps, companies and workers raised prices and wages more quickly. And why not? Excessive prices and wages wouldn't matter in a permanent boom. As for competitiveness, why worry?

Quelling inflationary behavior has aided economic growth. Job fears have also reduced inflationary pressures by lowering wage demands. What economists call the "natural rate" of unemployment—the rate at which labor bottlenecks trigger wage inflation—may have dropped. A crude consensus had put it around 6 percent; but in 1995, unemployment averaged 5.6 percent with (as yet) no sharp rise of inflation. Every 0.1 point shaved off the "natural" rate means an additional 130,000 jobs. Uncertainty about the future may temper the excesses—overborrowing or overspending—that trigger slumps.

None of this means that there won't be future recessions (there will), that all downsizing is justified (it isn't), or that some workers don't suffer terribly (they do). But in a market economy, job loss is unavoidable, and the social harm may be muted if layoffs are spread out and not concentrated—as in the past—in slumps or periods of industry crisis. Fired workers can be rehired more quickly in a growing economy. The *Times* visits Dayton, Ohio, where "everything, seemingly, is in upheaval," in part because NCR (absorbed into AT&T) is downsizing. Belatedly, we learn that the county unemployment rate is only 4.8 percent. Contrast that with Flint, Michigan, in the early 1980s, when auto layoffs sent the jobless rate to 20 percent.

What's missing in this debate (and the *Times*'s series) is a sense of how jobs are created. Companies hire workers to make a profit; workers take jobs to make a living. If profitable hiring becomes too hard, firms won't do it; if being unemployed becomes too easy, people won't look for jobs. Europeans increasingly admire our flexibility, because their system—though outwardly more compassionate—stifles job creation. They have more generous jobless benefits, steeper payroll taxes (to pay for the benefits), more restrictions on firing, and higher unemployment. In Germany, the jobless rate is 10.3 percent and headed up.

What Europe teaches is that societies can't outlaw job insecurity, but they can inadvertently outlaw job creation. The *Times* ignores Europe's experience and our own recent experiment with economic security as if they're irrelevant. Our system isn't perfect, but we shouldn't trash it unless we know how to improve it. We don't.

Newsweek
March 25, 1996

GOD IS IN THE DETAILS

We sometimes need a tiny theory to simplify life's large complexities. In that spirit, I christen this column "The God of Small Things," after the novel by the Indian writer Arundhati Roy. I do this because the title is more inviting than my actual subject—the triumph of "microeconomics." The idea is to explain the stark contrasts in economic performance around the world: everything from America's boom to Europe's high unemployment to Japan's stagnation. You can also throw in some other hot topics, such as the debate over Microsoft. The connections among them all exist through microeconomics.

It's a mouthful; so is its cousin "macroeconomics." But the concepts are simple. Microeconomics is the study of individual markets; it explores how consumers, workers, and companies behave in specific situations. By contrast, macroeconomics studies the entire economy; it examines rising (or falling) production, employment, and prices. When I took basic college economics in the 1960s, macroeconomics was the rage. It promised that by altering taxes, spending, and interest rates, government could keep the economy at or near "full employment." This was big picture; it was glorious. Microeconomics was little picture. It was tedious. Who cared about how the steel industry worked?

What we've learned is that the little picture is the big picture. Microeconomics deals with incentives. If people and companies face incentives to do stupid (or smart) things, they will do stupid (or smart) things. If many people face the same incentives, they will do the same stupid or smart things. And what people do collectively then shapes how an entire economy behaves. Europe's high unemployment (10 percent) is no mystery. Generous government benefits reward the jobless for staying idle. High payroll taxes and minimum wages discourage companies from hiring by raising labor costs. Cartels and regulation deter business start-ups and the ensuing job creation.

"Europe is back," said *The Wall Street Journal* last week. Well, just a bit. Unemployment is edging down. But as the *Journal* notes, the improvement is concentrated in countries that have removed restrictions. Germany (unemployment: 10 percent) and France (unemployment: 12 percent) remain "the laggards." France's latest idea to solve its jobless problem is to reduce the work week from 39 to 35 hours. If you cut hours and not pay, you increase the cost of labor. This will not ultimately create jobs.

As a practical matter, good macroeconomics—budget and interest rate policies—cannot easily offset bad microeconomics. Otherwise Europe's unemployment rate would be 5 percent. Japan teaches the same lesson. Its stagnation stems from qualities once thought to be strengths: high saving and low consumption. (Japan saves about 30 percent of its national income, twice the U.S. rate.) The trouble is that Japan recently hasn't used its huge savings well. In 1996, reports the Organization for Economic Cooperation and Development, the rate of return on invested capital was 13 percent in Japan and 28 percent in the United States. In Japan, banks lend to companies, and the two exist in cozy alliances—including cross-holdings of stock—that preclude each from being tough on the other.

Writes economist Edward Lincoln of the Brookings Institution: "Bankers . . . developed elaborate personal contacts lubricated by years of wining and dining." A society that can't invest well and penalizes consumption (through price-raising cartels and government rules) invites stagnation. Again, macroeconomic policies can't easily compensate. Japan's budget deficits are big; its interest rates are barely above zero. Last week, the government announced a $30 billion tax cut to spur the economy. It met with skepticism about how much good it will do.

The lesson is that small incentives (for good or ill) have large consequences. One common error in thinking about these matters is to equate capitalism—the private ownership of business—with "free markets." Few advanced societies have pure capitalism or totally free markets. Taxes and regulations curb businesses. Local culture interferes. As in Japan and Europe, private ownership can coexist with markets that act perversely.

The secret of the U.S. economy is that despite many flaws, its amalgam of incentives still operates constructively. Companies face competitive pressures to improve products and profits; people generally do better by working than loafing; the urge to "make it" spurs creativity. Still, some thorny societal problems involve microeconomics. Consider health care. Americans want to control costs; they also think that people should get the care they need. Fee-for-service medicine, underwritten by private or government insurance, produced a cost explosion; doctors and hospitals had no incentive to hold down spending. But managed care seems to create incentives to restrain costs by denying care. Somehow we need incentives that reconcile our ethical and economic demands. It may be impossible.

The Microsoft debate is also about microeconomics: how best to promote innovation? Microsoft contends that Windows has triumphed because computer users prefer a common standard. Microsoft says that if government antitrust actions impede it from adding new features to Windows, consumers will suffer. Government will dampen the incentive to innovate. Microsoft's critics claim the opposite: Windows's dominance stifles competition. It's ever harder to beat Microsoft even with superior applications software (because Microsoft can tie its programs to Windows or sell at cheap prices). So firms won't try. Who's right?

Good question. The story of economics over the past three decades is, in some ways, a recognition that questions like this count. The lure of macroeconomics lay in the illusion that it could make the whole system go smoothly almost regardless of how the economy's underlying sectors functioned. This was bound to disappoint. It's as if a car could run at breakneck speed even if the engine was corroded and missing some parts. What we know now is what we should have known all along: God lies in the details.

Newsweek
April 20, 1998

THE AGE OF FRIEDMAN

It is only in the past 10 or 15 years that Milton Friedman has been seen for what he is: the most influential living economist since World War II. For decades, Friedman—now 85 and long retired from the University of Chicago—was regarded as a brilliant outcast. He extolled "freedom," praised "free markets," and attacked big government. He was a cheerful dissenter in an era when government seemed the solution to most social problems. Confident of his views, Friedman would debate almost anyone, anywhere, but he was widely dismissed as a throwback.

Not anymore. Friedman's impact has been so huge that he's approaching John Maynard Keynes (1883–1946) as the century's most significant economist. He almost single-handedly resurrected the "quantity theory of money": the idea that inflation stems from "too much money chasing too few goods." Once governments accepted this, they could control inflation by slowing money growth. Abroad, Friedman has promoted market economics from Chile to China. At home, his ideas now permeate public debate. Even in the 1950s, he advocated a flat tax, school vouchers, and a "negative income tax" for the poor (embodied in today's earned income tax credit).

We now have Friedman's story of his odyssey from pariah to prophet in an autobiography written with his wife of nearly 60 years, Rose, *Two Lucky People* (University of Chicago Press, 1998). It is a remarkable tale of sheer doggedness.

Disapproval was so high in part because he never disguised his rejection of Keynes, who then mesmerized most economists. Where Keynes saw the private economy as highly unstable and therefore in need of governmental guidance, Friedman thought that government intervention often deepened economic slumps. Where Keynes toasted intellectuals and mocked capitalists—comparing the stock market, for example, to a "casino"—Friedman saw individual creativity as the wellspring of social progress. The contempt of many intellectuals for capitalism struck him as self-indulgent: biting the hand that fed them.

Like many postwar economists, Friedman has viewed economics as a "science"—much like physics—in which basic truths can be proved with evidence. As it happens, much of his scholarly work has discredited Keynesian economics. In 1957, he published *A Theory of the Consumption Function,* which refuted a central Keynesian tenet: that people spend less of their income—and save more—as societies grow wealthier. This presumably occurred because people's wants were satisfied. If true, it would justify higher government spending to offset weak private spending. But by analyzing historic consumption patterns, Friedman showed it wasn't true. People always developed new wants.

More important was his explanation of the Great Depression. In the 1930s, Keynes had argued the private economy could drop into a deep slump from which it might not automatically recover. In 1963, Friedman and Anna Schwartz published *A Monetary History of the United States,* contending that, on the contrary, the Depression resulted from governmental errors. Between 1929 and 1933, about 10,000 banks failed, leading to a one-third drop in the money supply and widespread bankruptcies. But Congress had created the

Federal Reserve in 1913 to prevent banking panics, Friedman and Schwartz noted. If the Fed had done its job, the Depression would have been only a normal business slump.

Finally, in 1968, Friedman conceived (simultaneously with economist Edmund Phelps of Columbia) of the "natural rate of unemployment." Until then, Keynesian dogma held that a bit less unemployment would bring only a bit more inflation and that the two could coexist in a stable relationship—say, 4 percent unemployment with 4 percent inflation. This implied that governments could select the most desirable mix of unemployment and inflation. Not so, said Friedman. If government tried to push unemployment below its "natural rate," inflation would rise ever higher. This ultimately described the pursuit of "full employment" in the 1960s and 1970s: inflation went from 1 percent in 1960 to 13 percent in 1979.

Friedman's influence also reflects his success as a popularizer. In 1962, he published *Capitalism and Freedom,* which described his then heretical views. In 1966, he was invited (along with two other prominent economists) to write a column for *Newsweek;* he did so until 1984. In 1980, he hosted a ten-part public television series entitled *Free to Choose* and wrote a book (with Rose, also an economist) by the same name. They condemned, among other things, welfare dependency and centrally planned economies.

Despite his advocacy, Friedman doubts that intellectuals can initiate political change. The "tyranny" of the status quo is too strong. "Only a crisis—actual or perceived—produces real change," he once wrote. Then "the actions that are taken depend on the ideas that are lying around." So he has sprinkled about "alternatives to existing policies." Crisis also remade his image. As inflation rose, he became more respectable. Communism's collapse vindicated his harsh view of central planning.

Two Lucky People chronicles this story, but as autobiography it is disappointing—a rambling book that lacks introspection. It never asks the central question: How did Friedman become Friedman?

By all odds, he belonged on the political Left. Born to two poor

Russian Jewish immigrants, Friedman grew up in Rahway, New Jersey. The family lived above a clothing store that his mother maintained, while his father worked in Manhattan. He recalls their arguing often over money. Public institutions treated him well. The local library helped make him a voracious reader; a high school civics teacher rates lavish praise; he attended Rutgers University on a public scholarship. He graduated in 1932 at the depth of the Depression, when political pressures pushed students to the Left.

Two Lucky People hardly explains how, given this climate, Friedman emerged by the early 1940s with an outlook so out of tune with the times. In conversation, he says that after Rutgers "I was mildly socialistic"—much like millions of other young people. He attributes his change to graduate study at the University of Chicago, where a cadre of economists did not accept the common view of the Depression as an inevitable crisis of capitalism. His government service during World War II—working on tax policy and a variety of weapons problems—may also have played a part. He felt the thrill of Washington but also saw firsthand the "manipulation, dishonesty, and self-seeking" of politics.

Some biographer may unravel this and other puzzles. Friedman's skepticism of government has never been total hostility. He has consistently seen a role for government in everything from reducing poverty to promoting education. But he has favored policies that checked government power and emphasized private responsibility. Though called a "conservative," Friedman disdains the label and sees himself as a libertarian or "radical"—someone who so prizes freedom that he would make dramatic political changes to enhance it. A true conservative, by contrast, only reluctantly alters existing social arrangements. Friedman's ambitions have never been so modest.

Newsweek
June 15, 1998

SHADES OF THE 1920s?

We know that today's economic boom will someday end, because all booms do. Yet faith in its immortality seems to grow almost daily. You see it in the stock market, confidence indexes, and tight labor markets. Has there ever been anything like it? Well, how about the 1920s?

The suggestion seems antisocial. It raises the specter of another Great Depression (unemployment averaged 18 percent in the 1930s). This need not be, of course, but peering back is still instructive. It teaches at least two important lessons: People do get carried away; and today's economy may have some little-noticed weaknesses.

Parallels between the 1920s and the 1990s abound. Then as now, the stock market soared. Then as now, new technologies dazzled. Today it's personal computers and the Internet. Then it was radios and mass-produced cars. Between 1919 and 1930, the number of radios went from almost zero to 14 million; car registrations tripled to 23 million. Then as now, people thought that the economy had permanently changed for the better. The 1920s supposedly heralded a "new era"; enlightened corporate managers meant more humane capitalism. The operative phrase in the 1990s is "the new paradigm." It holds that favorable forces (computers, foreign competition, deregulation) have made the economy more competitive, more productive, and more stable.

The economy is now said to lack the "excesses" that typically trigger a recession. Inflation is low; there isn't much obvious business overinvestment (in, say, office buildings). But this overlooks the stock market, which may be just such an "excess." It may be nudging the economy along by bolstering consumer confidence and spending. Higher stock prices, it seems, embolden people to spend more of their incomes. They feel wealthier. Or they cash in—and spend— some market profits. The extra spending sustains the expansion.

Consider. As the market has risen, the personal savings rate has fallen. In 1992, it was 6.2 percent of disposable income; by 1997, it had sunk to 3.8 percent, the lowest since at least 1946. And why shouldn't consumers feel cocky? The market's surge now rivals the 1920s runup as history's greatest. Ned Davis Research Inc. dates the present bull market to October 11, 1990, when the Dow Jones Industrial Average was at 2365.10. Since then, it's risen 288 percent (based on the April 17 close of 9167.50). In the 1920s, stocks rose 345 percent between October 1923 and September 1929.

Put another way, stock prices have almost quadrupled in value since 1990. On October 11, 1990, Ford closed at a little less than $10 a share; now it trades just under $50. Over the same period, Intel has risen from not quite $4 a share to the mid-$70s. (Prices reflect stock splits.) This has meant an explosion of personal stock wealth. At year-end 1990, the value of households' stock holdings was $3.1 trillion. By 1997, that was $11.4 trillion. (These figures include stocks owned directly and those held through mutual funds, retirement accounts, and pensions.)

But suppose the runaway market is (as the *Economist* said last week) a speculative "bubble." Suppose investors are simply chasing higher prices. Or suppose that something—Asia's economic crisis?—unexpectedly hurts profits. What then? Perhaps this: Stocks ultimately drop; confidence—bolstered by their rise—sags with their fall; consumer spending weakens or maybe declines. Consumer spending represents about 68 percent of the economy's output. If it weakens, corporate investment might be excessive; cutbacks could occur. The point is that the stock market isn't merely an indicator of the economy's performance. The market also determines how the economy behaves through mass psychology and consumer spending.

Although the connections between the market and the economy are uncertain, they have grown in the 1990s—just as in the 1920s—because stock wealth has soared and ownership has spread. It is creeping down from its bastion among the rich and upper middle class. Among families with incomes between $10,000 and $25,000, stock ownership rose from 13 to 25 percent between 1989 and 1995, reports the Federal Reserve. For families with incomes between $25,000 and $50,000, ownership went from 33 to 48 percent. And wealth effects are huge. In 1990, households' real estate wealth (mainly homes) totaled $6.6 trillion, more than twice stock wealth. By 1997, stock wealth was about 30 percent more than real estate wealth of $8.7 trillion.

In the late 1920s, warnings that the market was overvalued didn't deflate the mania. One reason is that until early 1928, the market's rise reflected higher profits and dividends. Most of the 1990s surge also rests on solid economic gains. Inflation and interest rates have declined; this makes stocks worth more, because competing interest-bearing investments (bonds, bank deposits) are less attractive. And profits have doubled since 1990, boosting stocks.

But the market has moved well beyond present profits. Its price/earnings ratio (P/E)—the price of an average stock divided by its average per share earnings—is now at an historical high of 28. Since World War II, PEs have averaged about 14. Something much higher may now be warranted. But 28?

Who knows? Perhaps higher prices will ultimately be vindicated by economic conditions (lower interest rates, higher profits). Even if stocks dropped 15 or 20 percent now, investors and consumers might take the decline in stride. After all, stock prices would still be where they were in early 1997 and more than twice their early 1991 level. And the 1990s are not the 1920s. Although the Crash of 1929 (the Dow dropped 48 percent between September and mid-November) did mark the start of a sharp recession, it did not cause the Depression. The Depression occurred because the Federal Reserve didn't do its job: it allowed 11,000 banks to become insolvent by 1933; and it permitted the money supply to drop by a third. These were preventable events that would probably now be prevented.

It's dangerous to overdo historical analogies. We cannot predict the future by consulting the past. So the 1920s can't tell us whether today's boom will end next week, next month, or even next year. Nor does it say whether the end will come with a loud thud or a quiet whimper. But the history is mighty intriguing and leaves a sobering question. The economy has surely changed since 1929, but has human nature?

The Washington Post
April 22, 1998

SPIRIT OF ADAM SMITH

Adam Smith (1723–1790) is a man for our time—or ought to be. This is less because he championed free markets than because he cared about so much more than free markets. What concerned Smith was constructing a decent society. Free markets were only one means to that end. Government was another, and Smith constantly probed the proper roles for government and the market. Smith was long on wisdom, short on self-righteousness. We could use his spirit today, because we seem to have arrived at the opposite mix: surplus self-righteousness and scarce wisdom.

Liberals are so protective of government that they cannot concede the great power of Smith's "invisible hand." Self-interest is not simply greed, selfishness, or narcissism. If properly constrained, it is an immense force for social good, and much human progress stems from the independent exertions and creative energies of individuals and enterprises. Liberals recoil at this notion because it deprives them of the power, social status, and psychological gratification of seeming to deliver (through government) all the trappings of the good society.

Meanwhile, conservatives are so contemptuous of government that they cannot admit that it is often more than a necessary evil. It creates the legal and political framework without which tolerably free markets could not survive. It also supplies the collective services—from defense to roads—that the private market doesn't and deals with the market's unwanted "excesses." Smith realized that government produced these benefits, but many conservatives who cite him seem oblivious to their existence or importance.

I don't claim to have read Smith's *The Wealth of Nations* (1776) from cover to cover. But anyone who doubts the complexity of his thinking ought to plunge into a short but superb intellectual biography by historian Jerry Muller of Catholic University (*Adam Smith in His Time and Ours,* Princeton University Press). In it, he demolishes the stereotype of Smith as an antigovernment zealot. That image founders on one fact: Smith served for years as a bureaucrat, Scotland's commissioner of customs. He collected import duties, then the government's largest source of revenue. The job was akin to the head of the IRS today.

Smith's theories explained changes that had already occurred. In eighteenth-century Britain, feudalism had collapsed. Farm production rose, as did living standards. In England, people felt ashamed to go without shoes; in France, being shoeless was still common. Blankets, linens, and ironware became common in England. Smith attributed the new wealth to the triumph of the market: buying and selling. Before, food was consumed mostly by those who produced it or their feudal lords. Manufacturing was also transformed. "Goods once produced laboriously at home—clothes, beer, candles . . . furniture—could now be purchased," writes Muller.

The market multiplied wealth, Smith reasoned, because it led to economic specialization: the "division of labor" that—through more knowledge, experience, and customized machinery—raised production. None of this was planned. It flowed (as if by an invisible hand) from the striving of sellers to maximize their wealth. "It is not from the benevolence of the butcher, the brewer, or the baker, that we expect our dinner," Smith wrote memorably, "but from their regard to their own interest."

Smith grasped that incentives count: that is, how people are motivated and toward what ends. The lesson endures. Similar peoples with dissimilar incentives—embedded in national policies—fare differently, as economist Mancur Olson of the University of Maryland says: "[In] most of the postwar period, China, Germany and Korea have been divided. . . . The economic performances of Hong Kong and Taiwan, of West Germany, and of South Korea have been [incomparably] better than [those] of mainland China, East Germany and North Korea."

Government's ability to cripple the market appalled Smith. *The Wealth of Nations* aimed to fortify legislators against "the pressures of economic groups" for special privileges, Muller says. But Smith's skepticism of government wasn't a revulsion for it. He "enjoyed the work" as customs commissioner, writes Muller. This was not hypocrisy, because Smith saw three vital roles for government: 1) providing defense; 2) ensuring justice and protecting property; and 3) building roads, canals, harbors—"infrastructure." Government had to be properly financed.

Nor did Smith believe that wealth was all that mattered. Quite the opposite. He wanted a society that would be less violent and more civil—one that tempered people's worst "passions." Greater wealth, by relieving suffering, enabled people to be more "benevolent." And though the market could be cruel and crass, it also encouraged stable commercial relations. That was a civilizing influence, Smith argued. Finally, Smith believed in the primacy of the family as a moral force (the place where children learn self-control) and as a source of personal happiness.

Deciding what government should do is harder in our era than Smith's precisely because its activities—ranging from the social safety net to environmental regulation—are so much greater. But his pragmatic approach, unburdened by dogma and sensitive to how people (and institutions) actually behave, is more needed than ever.

He assigned social tasks where he thought they could best be met, whether that be the market or government. By contrast, today's liberals often assume that the "market is wasteful or immoral," writes Muller. Ignoring how government can harm incentives—killing initiative, creating dependence—they often substitute "good intentions for sound policies."

As for conservatives, their use of Smith ignores what he said about the defects of markets. He supported, for example, universal education as an antidote to the numbing effects of economic specialization. Is it any wonder that our debates seem so unsatisfying? The antagonists talk past each other. Smith combined a lofty vision of a decent society with an exacting analysis of the means of attaining it. Our modern luminaries often assume that their means are always up to their ends.

The Washington Post
November 27, 1996

PART IV

BUSINESS

IN PRAISE OF PARKINSON

Let us now praise Parkinson. That's C. Northcote Parkinson, the British historian who coined Parkinson's Law: Work expands so as to fill the time available for its completion. This is one of the stunning insights of our time, and yet when Parkinson died the other day at 83, America's major newspapers barely noted his passing. *The Washington Post* buried his obit on page B7. *The New York Times* stuck it on page A19. Boo, and double boo. What a lousy sense of history.

We live in an age of bureaucracy. We all work for big companies, Big Government, big universities, big media, big hospitals—or have to deal with them. Parkinson was our most penetrating (and funniest) observer of bureaucracy. How could he be so casually dismissed? Maybe because his truths, once revealed, are so obvious that they seem less impressive than more esoteric axioms that, on inspection, usually aren't true.

Every passing day confirms Parkinson's relevance. Successful bureaucrats, he said, are driven by two guiding forces: 1) "to multiply subordinates, not rivals"; and 2) "to make work for each other."

Every official who feels overworked appoints subordinates, who (feeling overworked) do likewise. Bureaucracies left to themselves—that is, left to create make-work—ultimately self-destruct. They become immobilized and can't adapt to change. Witness the collapse of the Soviet Union and (a lesser example) the turmoil at General Motors.

We also learn from Parkinson why deadlines are essential. Because work can be endlessly elastic, nothing would ever get done without deadlines. If this column were not due today, I would be writing it tomorrow. And the next day, and the next. I would write it forever, because there would be forever to write it. Deadlines may inspire superficial thought, but without deadlines there would be no thought at all.

Some of Parkinson's scholarly works (*British Intervention in Malaya, 1867 to 1877*) aren't inviting. His reputation rests mainly on *Parkinson's Law* (1957) and its successor, *The Law and the Profits* (1960). These books brim with wisdom and merriment. No committee can succeed with more than 21 members. At that point, "it is hopeless. It is dead." It will produce only "drivel." A few committee members may quietly "exchange little notes that read, 'Lunch with me tomorrow—we'll fix it then.' "

At meetings, people talk in inverse proportion to how much they know, Parkinson observed. Those who don't know much can blab endlessly and exhaust all their knowledge during the span of a meeting. They are not inhibited by ignorance, because they don't know what they don't know. By contrast, the well informed can't possibly explain everything during one meeting. Anything they might say would insult others by exposing their ignorance. A bad career move. Better to shut up.

Every successful career, Parkinson explained, passes through ten stages:

1. Age of Qualification (three years)
2. Age of Discretion (seven years)
3. Age of Promotion (five years)

4. Age of Responsibility (three years)
5. Age of Authority (seven years)
6. Age of Achievement (nine years)
7. Age of Distinction (six years)
8. Age of Dignity (three years)
9. Age of Wisdom (seven years)
10. Age of Obstruction (?)

However, many careers start successfully and then finish badly:

6. Age of Frustration (nine years)
7. Age of Jealousy (four years)
8. Age of Resignation (five years)
9. Age of Oblivion (?)

Parkinson's Second Law, though not as well known as the first, is almost as important: Expenditure rises to meet income. He also added a qualification: Expenditure not only rises to meet income, but tends to surpass it. Translation: The more you have, the more you want. This explains why the wealthy are not always happy or even solvent. A few years back, a couple of the Texas Hunt brothers (who had been billionaires) went bankrupt trying to corner the world silver market. They should have read Parkinson.

But Parkinson mainly intended his second law to explain the constant rise in government spending. Governments, he said, would spend whatever they had—and perhaps a bit more. Raise taxes and you raise spending. Lower taxes and you might lower spending. Alas, the qualification to Parkinson's Second Law may be more valid than the law. Governments (especially ours) show little embarrassment in spending well beyond their taxes.

Parkinson liked to quote Thomas Jefferson on the value of small government. "I regard economy [in government] among the first and most important virtues," Jefferson said. Without it, "we must be taxed in our meat and our drink, in our necessities and comforts, in our labor and in our amusements." And finally: "If we can prevent the Government from wasting the labor of the people, under the pretense of caring for them, they will be happy." (President Clinton, an eager spender, poses as an heir of Jefferson. Parkinson would have said: "Surely, sir, you jest.")

Our debt to Parkinson exceeds his own insights. He inspired imitators, who have devised other—if lesser—laws of life. For example, the Peter Principle ("Every employee tends to rise to his level of incompetence"). I was about to put Murphy's Law ("If it can go wrong, it will") in this category, but on checking, I discover that this law came earlier, in 1949. Its author was Ed Murphy, an aircraft engineer. Referring to a technician, Murphy said: "If there is any way to do it wrong, he will."

Oh, well. Parkinson isn't the font of all wisdom. Just a lot. As a Brit, he "regarded most Americans as illiterate," said the *Times* of London in its obituary. We can forgive him this, because he helped us understand and made us laugh. Thanks, pal.

The Washington Post
March 17, 1993

BUREAUCRACY AS LIFE

When William H. Whyte Jr.'s *The Organization Man* appeared 30 years ago, his publisher thought it would be a bust. The first printing was tiny. But soon after the book went on sale in December 1956, it hit the bestseller list and stayed there for seven months. Whyte had touched a responsive chord in postwar Americans. Although these graduates of the Depression basked in prosperity, they were uneasy. Somehow they had lost—and they weren't quite sure how—some of their freedom to Big Business, Big Government, and Big Everything.

The Organization Man survives as a modern classic because it captures a permanent part of our social condition. We recognize gigantic organizations as inevitable, even desirable, and yet we mistrust them. But along with the mistrust is a longing for the organizations' psychic and economic shelter. There is something in most of us that draws pride, status, and companionship from affiliation with a larger group.

Whyte obviously was not the first analyst of bureaucracies. His insight lay in understanding that their dangers often reflected their strengths. Writing when faith in large organizations was at its zenith, he worried precisely because bureaucracies generally worked well and were necessary. They made the toothpaste, sold the insurance, provided education, and collected taxes. Because the organization seemed sensible and could offer good pay, job security, and prestige, its demands on the individual might prove irresistible. They would stifle choice and creativity.

"It is not so much that the Organization is going to push the individual around more than it used to," Whyte wrote. "It is that it is becoming increasingly hard for the individual to figure out when he is being pushed around."

With hindsight, of course, we know that Whyte's vision was overdrawn. The organization's advance was never as relentless as he imagined. Some bureaucracies are just that—bureaucracies in the worst sense. The giant corporation's control of the economy has never been complete. Outsiders have always had the chance to fashion new enterprises from scratch. In the 1950s, Ray Kroc opened his first McDonald's, Joseph Wilson launched the Xerox machine, and Ken Olsen created Digital Equipment Corp., to name but three midgets that became giants.

The giants also falter. Who imagined that American Telephone & Telegraph would one day decide to lay off 27,000 workers? Or that General Motors would have to cut its white-collar workforce by 25 percent? In a sense, the implicit contract that Whyte worried would bribe Americans into passivity has frayed at both ends. On the one side, the big corporation is less able to provide good pay and job security. On the other, worker loyalty is fading.

Popular culture has absorbed Whyte's heresy. To be cynical about corporate motives is now normal, even chic. The awe in which large organizations were held in the mid-1950s reflected fleeting circumstances. It was not merely the yearning of a war-weary Depression-era generation for prosperity. World War II itself had seemed to vindicate big organizations: the military, wartime industry, and government agencies. More than 16 million Americans had been in uniform. Everyone knew big organizations exacted a price, but the price seemed worth it. The war had been won.

But, as Whyte wrote, this consensus was cracking. In 1955, *The Man in the Gray Flannel Suit* became a bestseller. In 1960, *The Apartment* won the Academy Award for best picture. Each ridiculed corporate regimentation. Attitudes were changing. Still, the shift hasn't erased the conflict between the individual and the organization. For many, career jobs remain the norm. By their late 30s, about half of men have jobs that last 20 years or longer. And fringe benefits, which tie people to jobs even if they prefer to move, have grown with time. In the 1950s, pensions and health insurance were in their infancy.

Whyte himself did not condemn the superficial trappings of social conformity, including its newest symbol in the 1950s: suburban tract housing. Prosperity was not evil, he contended, and mass production inevitably created some uniformity. Nor did *The Organization Man* pine for the "rugged individual," who (Whyte argued) was not a realistic model in a bureaucratic world. Whyte's vaguer ideal of individualism meant controlling "one's destiny."

What he rejected was a social philosophy that left this task to the organization. In the 1950s, Americans were being told—and accepting, Whyte thought—that submitting to the organization's demands was social progress. The large organization was society's "source of creativity." Cooperation advanced the greater good. Meanwhile, the caring organization would create "a *harmonious* atmosphere [that] . . . will bring out the best in everyone."

The irony today is that U.S. companies are criticized—compared with, say, Japanese firms—for not inspiring enough cooperation. To Whyte, though, the picture of placid fulfillment was phony. He conceded that the organization needed cooperation but argued that the individual's needs were always subordinate to the organization's larger purposes. Therein lay the dilemma. Most people, dependent on an organization, had to choose how much to accept its demands and how much to assert their individuality. What to do was rarely clear. Was resisting "being courageous—or just stubborn? Help-ful—or selfish? [Who was] right after all?"

Most of us live with the daily ambiguities and compromises that stem from this reality. Perhaps in Japan, where group loyalties are stronger, the tensions are muted. In our culture, they are acute. *The Organization Man* has lasting relevance because it recognizes their permanence. Some organizations are better and some are worse. But Whyte rejected the congenital American optimism that denies conflicts and imagines all stories having happy endings. He found the management fads and psychological theorems that promised blissful utopias—they were as common in the 1950s as they are today—to be shallow and self-serving. He wrote: "But what is the '*solution*'? many ask. There is no solution." This was true 30 years ago, and it's still true.

Newsweek
January 12, 1987

THE SOVEREIGN CONSUMER

We all owe the folks at the Coca-Cola Co. a debt of gratitude. They've provided us with free summertime entertainment and—just coincidentally—an elementary lesson in the mechanics of modern capitalism. They have infused new meaning into an old concept: consumer sovereignty.* They have shown that even the most successful corporations, for all their elaborate marketing surveys and lavish advertising, remain hostage to often unpredictable consumer habits, lifestyles, and desires.

I know that's hard to swallow. The idea that huge corporations manipulate us is deeply ingrained in popular culture. We see ourselves as the reluctant wards of America's megafirms. Indeed, the Coke furor fed on the victim mentality. It was less a flavor crusade than an anticorporate rebellion: an issue simple and symbolic enough to concentrate our vague anticorporate hostilities against a

---

* Coca-Cola had tried to change the formula of basic Coke. Despite intensive market research (which seemed to prove the greater popularity of the new formula) and massive advertising, consumers decisively rejected the new formula. Coke returned its classic formula to the market.

single target. It was satisfying (even if you don't drink Coke) precisely because it relieved a mass urge to yell, "Up the organization"—and get some results.

Gee, it felt good.

But the error is mistaking our usual helplessness for corporate power. If the transmission on your General Motors car fails, you want Roger Smith (GM's chairman) to fix it. Although Smith's unavailability makes GM seem imperious, it does not make GM omnipotent. Consumer sovereignty often exercises itself impersonally and invisibly. Taken together, changing technologies and new businesses, as well as shifting lifestyles and values, prevent existing companies from controlling what we want—and what they can sell. What was exceptional about the Coca-Cola episode was that the consumer voice was so direct and (for Coke's executives) so humiliating.

The "market" simply signifies a system of trial and error. Unless firms can suppress choice and change, they ultimately remain the market's prisoners. This doesn't mean we have all the daily choices we might like. But the most vital choices (and the most threatening forms of competition) are often those involving broad economic, technological, and social changes beyond corporate control. For example, today's bestselling consumer appliance, the microwave oven (estimated 1985 sales: 10 million units), has benefited from the rise of two-income families with scarce cooking time.

The idea that corporations manipulate markets dates back to the 1950s, when economist John Kenneth Galbraith argued that advertising creates wants that people don't have. Therefore firms can bend consumer choice to accommodate technology. The idea's glib appeal seems vindicated by today's high-tech marketing. Since the 1970 census, for example, the government has made available computer tapes with key demographic data—population, income, age, marital status, education—by ZIP code. When combined with other polling data on buying habits or values, market researchers can construct neighborhood profiles to target direct mail, assess (or create) advertising, or select store locations.

But all this confers only an aura of control.

The notion that advertising creates wants is inane, as sociologist Michael Schudson shows in a new book (*Advertising, the Uneasy Persuasion,* Basic Books). Some products—from cocaine to many generic goods—succeed with little or no advertising. Schudson also examined what was considered an advertising-induced explosion in the 1920s of cigarette smoking, especially among women. In fact, the growth mostly reflected men switching from chewing tobacco and cigars. And nonadvertising factors were the driving forces: milder tobacco blends made cigarettes easier to try; cigarettes given to soldiers in World War I constituted a massive promotion; and rising urbanization discouraged tobacco chewing.

Mostly, advertising influences brand selection, not consumption patterns. "Any new consumer product that does not disappear quickly," Schudson writes, "is probably related to deep social currents." Schudson is no advertising apologist. He dislikes much of it and thinks some consumers (especially children) vulnerable to its excesses. But he also finds its powers exaggerated.

Why? First, people don't pay attention; one 1981 study put television ad recall at 7 percent. Second, they get confused; in another study a third of viewers praising Kodak cited ads done by Polaroid. Finally, they're skeptical; a 1980 survey found 70 percent of Americans concerned about advertising's truthfulness. In the end, price, personal experience, and word-of-mouth referrals are more vital than advertising to commercial success. If advertising were essential to promote increasingly artificial wants, relative advertising spending ought to rise; in fact it was 2.3 percent of gross national product in both 1937 and 1983.

As for all that marketing data, it can't infallibly predict what people will buy. Coke's blunder and other marketing flubs are portrayed as isolated failures. Actually, they're not. Only two of every three new products succeed, according to Booz, Allen & Hamilton; and for every success, at least seven ideas are studied. Consumers constantly surprise. The explosion of videocassette recorder sales (and all the related industries) stunned most manufacturers. If markets remain open, consumer sovereignty and corporate giantism can coexist. A corporate titan, Procter & Gamble, pioneered disposable diapers in 1961; today, 16 billion are sold in the United States annually, covering an estimated three-quarters of diapering. They're expensive (about 17 cents apiece), and they've triumphed because parents prefer them.

Our sense of servitude to corporate America in part reflects self-doubts about our consumer society. Should we really want all the things we apparently do? The mystique of corporate power is also reinforced by its acceptance by both the corporation's propagandists (who romanticize its marketing acumen) and its social critics (who deplore its size and remoteness). Well, maybe they're right. Maybe I'm wrong about consumer sovereignty. Maybe the folks at Coca-Cola engineered a giant hoax. Maybe they always planned to reintroduce "classic" Coke. Maybe it was a ploy to generate free publicity. Maybe they gladly made themselves look like buffoons. If so, my hat's off to them. They did a great job.

Newsweek
July 29, 1985

IN PRAISE OF McDONALD'S

I am thrilled. The McDonald's located a block from my office has reopened. Ever since it closed two years ago—the building was torn down—I have suffered cruelly. Now I can get my Big Mac and fries again. My writing has definitely improved.

Celebrating a company for its own sake is a journalistic no-no: a bit of crass commercialism that's professionally uncool. I don't care. McDonald's is no ordinary company. It's the greatest restaurant chain in history. A recent survey of the country's best-known brands put McDonald's in the top five (Coca-Cola was number one). McDonald's remains one of the fascinating phenomena of our times. Among other things, McDonald's

• serves about one-third of all the hamburgers sold in U.S. restaurants (the company's historical total of hamburgers now exceeds 70 billion).

• is so big (U.S. sales in 1988: $11.4 billion) that it's larger than the next three fast-food chains combined (Burger King, Kentucky Fried Chicken, and Pizza Hut).

• opens a new restaurant every 15 hours (the fastest growth

is abroad, with overseas sales accounting for nearly a third of McDonald's total).

There are three types of Americans. First are those who, like me, openly worship McDonald's. Next is a much larger group who like McDonald's but would never admit it. These people use their children as an excuse to go—or visit a McDonald's only where they won't be recognized by family and friends. Finally, there's a small group of weirdos who genuinely dislike McDonald's. They can't stand the food and regard McDonald's as the embodiment of all that is vulgar in American mass culture.

Before Ray Kroc—the man who made the chain what it is today—there were Richard and Maurice McDonald. The brothers McDonald conceived the golden arches and the basic ideas behind fast food. In 1948, they converted a successful conventional restaurant in San Bernardino, California, into the prototype of every subsequent fast-food restaurant. They shortened a long menu to five items (hamburgers, cheeseburgers, fries, milkshakes, and sodas). They cut prices (a hamburger went from 30 cents to 15 cents). And they adopted assembly-line cooking.

"Commercial cooking [had been] considered a personal art," writes John Love in his superb *McDonald's, Behind the Arches* (Bantam, 1986). "But the brothers' concept of a limited menu allowed them to break down food operations into simple, repetitive tasks that could be learned quickly. . . ." "Grill men" made the hamburgers, which were wrapped by "dressers." There were "shake men," "fry men," and the "countermen" who filled orders.

Kroc improved and franchised the brothers' system (they had flopped at expansion). He was fanatical about cleanliness, because he realized that dirty restaurants would kill family business. McDonald's set strict standards on everything from meat quality to frying potatoes. In 1961, it created Hamburger University to train managers. Field inspections were frequent. Suppliers that didn't meet standards were fired. Operators who deviated couldn't get additional franchises. "We will make conformists out of them in a hurry," Kroc said in 1958, three years after his first McDonald's.

I admit that the resulting food colossus has many uncharming aspects. The work is boring and demanding, although—as Ben Wildavsky writes in the Heritage Foundation's magazine—these jobs do teach vital employment skills: punctuality, teamwork, and customer courtesy. (Wildavsky estimates that one in 15 new workers now starts out at a McDonald's job.) The chain has been unimaginative in anticipating broader social concerns involving its business. Only now, for example, is it beginning an experimental recycling program for its plastic containers.

There's also an arrogant edge to McDonald's that reflects its combativeness and success. When a rival chain opened a store across from a McDonald's in the 1960s, the McDonald's man strode across the street and proclaimed: "We're going to run you out of business." That captures the corporate spirit. Even so, the McDonald's machine is not infallible. Assaulted by fast-food pizzas and tacos, traffic at many U.S. McDonald's has slipped slightly—something that rarely, if ever, has happened before.

Condemning McDonald's impersonal uniformity overlooks the deeper social changes in postwar society that created fast food. As Americans became more mobile and harried, people looked for something that was familiar, quick, and dependable. McDonald's uniformity and quality satisfied these needs. The same formula is now working abroad. At the end of September, 2,763 of the chain's 10,873 restaurants were foreign. There were 677 in Japan, 598 in Canada, and 303 in West Germany.

It's impossible to overstate the quality control. Once in Tokyo, I had a Big Mac. A Japanese Big Mac doesn't merely taste like an American Big Mac. It tastes exactly the same. Ditto for the fries. If you closed your eyes, you were back at your neighborhood McDonald's. Put another way: If other American companies had McDonald's quality control, Japanese exports to the United States would be half today's level.

In the end, McDonald's exemplifies what I have called "the Big Mac Principle." It holds that a Big Mac tastes better than "two all beef patties, special sauce, lettuce, cheese, pickles, onions on a sesame seed bun." The whole, in short, is greater than the sum of its parts. Or, if you think a Big Mac tastes worse than its ingredients, you have the Big Mac Principle in Reverse. Companies, politicians, sports teams, bosses, entire civilizations—in fact, almost anything—can be understood as either the Big Mac Principle or the Big Mac Principle in Reverse. Congress, for example, is the Big Mac Principle in Reverse.

Alas, my great insight has yet to receive its proper recognition. It surely ranks with Parkinson's Law or the Peter Principle. But at least the source of my inspiration is once again close at hand. Welcome back, McDonald's.

The Washington Post
November 1, 1989

CLOSE TO THE LUNATIC EDGE

I don't much like Coke, but I love Coca-Cola's annual report. It contains lots of intriguing information and business insights. It's also fun to read—mainly because its boundless exuberance for Coke is, well, a good chuckle and says a lot about the present obsessional quality of American management. Coke's is just one of the annual reports that I scan every spring, when most are issued. They are an overlooked form of social history and economic commentary.

In its report, for example, IBM says that the Internet's first major commercial use will be business-to-business purchasing; IBM reckons this market to be ten times larger than the consumer market. From Colgate-Palmolive we learn that in India annual use of toothpaste is only 67 grams per person, compared with a global average of 362 grams; as nations grow richer, their citizens brush more. Johnson & Johnson, the health products company, reminds us of the rapidity of economic change; last year 35 percent of the company's sales came from new products of the past five years.

These reports, of course, warrant skepticism. Their messages are selective (bad news drops to footnotes, if possible), and their tone is upbeat (few companies admit to bleak prospects or befuddled management). Still, they can instruct and entertain. Coca-Cola is probably the greatest brand name ever. The company claims that it sells nearly half (48 percent) of the world's soft drinks. It also estimates that this represents "less than 2 percent of the approximately 64 ounces of fluid human beings need every day." Roberto C. Goizueta, Coke's driven chairman, apparently regards the other 98 percent as fair game. He writes:

"The Coca-Cola Company is still unquenchably thirsty—thirsty for more ways to reach more consumers in more places with more of our products, creating more value for you [the shareholders] . . . truly, *we are just getting started.*" (The italics are in the original.) In the United States, individuals on average drink 363 Coca-Cola soft drinks a year—almost one a day. It's only five a year in China, nine in Indonesia, and thirteen in Russia. At another point, Goizueta puts Coke in grander perspective: "A billion hours ago, human life appeared on Earth. A billion minutes ago, Christianity emerged. A billion seconds ago, the Beatles changed music forever. A billion Coca-Colas ago was yesterday morning." (Translation: A billion Cokes are sold every two days.)

Fifty years ago reports weren't like this. The 1946 report of Bethlehem Steel ran to 33 pages, versus Coke's current 73 pages. The Bethlehem report had a gray cover, no pictures, and no charts. Coke's has a fire-engine-red cover and is splashed through with clever charts and graphics. The aim is to project corporate character, even charisma. And the boilerplate rhetoric is revealing; it illuminates prevailing management philosophy.

Bethlehem's 1946 report doesn't mention corporate purpose or social conditions except for a brief reference to strikes. In fact, 1946 was probably the most strike-prone year in U.S. history; one in eleven workers went out. But management was inarticulate and assumed that companies existed to make money. In the 1960s, the spirit shifted. "Companies caught on to the idea that an important reader group [for reports] was employees—you could communicate your beliefs, your ethics, your strategy," says William Bruns of the

Harvard Business School. And executives wanted to show they were socially responsible as well as efficient. Here's the American Can Co. in 1971:

"[In] our changing social contract . . . management must satisfy the legitimate needs of all three participating partners—our customers, our owners and our employees." By the mid-1980s, the tone shifted again. Institutional investors (pension funds, mutual funds) and security analysts had to be impressed. So today's champion slogan is "Creating shareholder value." This reemphasizes profitability as a goal that, if not satisfied, might mean corporate extinction. (American Can, for example, was merged out of existence.) Still, most companies also try to use their reports to humanize themselves by telling stories about their unsung heroes: their workers.

Every so often these stories transcend shrewd publicity devices or cheap rewards. In its report, Merck—the $20-billion drug company—recounts the decade-long history of Crixivan, a protease-inhibitor drug used to fight AIDS. The project suffered constant setbacks. In 1988, the lead researcher died in the bombing of Pan Am 103. Early versions repeatedly failed in clinical trials. Manufacturing of the drug was immensely complex; initially it took a year to make 100 pounds of the active ingredient. But by early 1996, the drug was approved, and by year-end, 125,000 patients were using it. The people who made this possible are spread across two pages of Merck's report.

I don't own stock in Merck or any other company mentioned in this column. But stories like this remind us that management—whatever it is—matters. Our well-being depends on it. The trouble is that annual reports never tell us conclusively whether a company is well managed. Is Microsoft? Just because it's hugely profitable isn't a guarantee. Microsoft's great advantage is that its main product (Windows) is so dominant in a fast-growing market that it generates vast amounts of cash that might camouflage or offset other management shortcomings. In 1996, Microsoft had $2.2 billion in profits on sales of $8.7 billion.

But these reports do tell us something of the psyche of the people atop major companies. There's a mix of anxiety about competition and bravado about performance. That may explain why so many U.S. companies still excel and why, also, so many CEOs feel entitled to their lavish (sometimes outlandish) pay. Their single-mindedness often verges on fanaticism. Jack Welch, the chairman of General Electric, said as much in a recent interview with Frank Swoboda of *The Washington Post.* Two decades ago, Welch said, being named CEO was the culmination of a career. Now "it's the beginning of a career," he said. "You cannot be a moderate, balanced, thoughtful, careful articulator of policy. You've got to be on the lunatic fringe."

Newsweek
April 21, 1997

THE AGING OF RALPH NADER

You can still find Ralph Nader working in cluttered offices about a 15-minute walk from the White House. There are bookcases filled with congressional debates and tables strewn with newspapers. Nader has aged well. At 51 he still looks much as he did 20 years ago, when publication of *Unsafe at Any Speed* thrust him into the public eye. He still favors plain, drab suits. His hair remains thick and closely cut. But there is gray around the ears, and his middle-aged thinness makes him seem a little haggard.

The most interesting thing about Nader these days is how uncontroversial he has become. In part, he mirrors our changing national mood. Americans, said Tocqueville, believe in the "indefinite perfectibility of man." Nader is proof of the durability—and fickleness—of that impulse. He flourished in the late 1960s and early 1970s, when confidence in our economic superiority was matched only by contempt for established authority. The fragile economy of the 1980s makes Nader a throwaway. Not only are we less eager for new regulatory forays, but our insecurity has fostered a narrow nationalism that often (and wrongly) views social criticism as an unpatriotic act.

But, mostly, Nader is a victim of his own success. Talk to him, and he hasn't changed. He quickly reverts to form, inveighing against Reagan and corporate executives. But the country has changed. Twenty years ago, the vague concepts of "social responsibility" and "consumerism" barely existed; now (diluted, to be sure) they are the conventional wisdom, even in business. Yes, Virginia, there's a Society of Consumer Affairs Professionals in Business with 1,400 members, up from 100 in 1973. And, Reagan notwithstanding, Nader's social regulation—of everything from auto safety to pollution—has triumphed. The boundaries of the market have been redrawn.

It is difficult now to recall the passions that Nader once aroused. In his heyday, he was a one-man conglomerate of outrage; he franchised his virtue. Hundreds of Nader's Raiders—mostly college students or recent graduates—poked into the affairs of business and government. By 1972, they had produced at least 14 books, on subjects ranging from antitrust to water pollution. Business leaders felt besieged. "He can . . . write books," Henry Ford II once snapped. "But I don't think he knows anything about engineering safety into automobiles." More than that, they saw Nader as a threat to capitalism.

Was he so menacing? Not really. He has never suggested a sweeping alternative to private property. He's always been a reformer, not a radical. The more the economy prospered, the more new demands fell on business. Today, the rationale for these demands is widely accepted: that profit-seeking firms sometimes cause social problems—pollution, for example—that the market doesn't correct. Indeed, it may frustrate correction. A firm that independently reduces pollution suffers a competitive disadvantage. Government regulation is justified.

Nader's best allies were his adversaries. After his blistering criticism of the Chevrolet Corvair, General Motors had him tailed by private investigators. Its subsequent public apology made Nader a national figure—and more. In effect, GM had ceded the high moral ground. If GM descended into the gutter, could anything business said be trusted? A 1966 *New Yorker* cartoon caught Nader's appeal. It showed a used-car salesman pointing at one of his wares and haranguing a customer: "I happen to know that Ralph Nader's mother drives this model."

Unwittingly, perhaps, Nader became a great political innovator. Just as Depression-era party loyalties were fading, he helped pioneer "issues" politics. He understood that its ammunition was information: detailed, accurate, and plentiful. It discredits your opponent and satisfies the mass media. He created advocacy groups that have been imitated on the Right and Left, by antiabortionists as well as environmentalists. His most tangible accomplishments are the laws that he—and many others—promoted, including the National Traffic and Motor Vehicle Safety Act (1966); the Clean Air Act (1970); the Clean Water Act (1972); and the Freedom of Information Act (1974).

Nader's luster had to fade, and not simply because he succeeded too well or the economy soured. His crusade suffered from arrogant excesses and obvious inconsistencies. Nader now lauds our energy efficiency—energy use in 1984 was less than in 1973, even though the economy's production was 30 percent greater—but he has deplored the higher energy prices that forced greater efficiency. At times, his investigations became trivial; a Nader-sponsored group once proposed probing junk food at sports arenas. More generally, the regulatory enterprise has lost its romanticism and has become technical. Are alleged social problems real? Are they worth correcting? If so, at what cost?

Nader is both the prisoner and creation of our culture. As an optimistic society, we weary of his endless discontents. We're uncomfortable with his personal brand of consumption. He doesn't own a car, home, or most appliances. He disapproves of wasteful or frivolous products, suggesting that the best choice is often "not buying at all." If Nader were typical, our economy would still be stuck in the 1920s. When he champions individual choice against corporate control, he's a hero; when he preaches his values, he's an alien priest.

We insist on individuality, even if it's mass-marketed; we want our Big Macs.

These are quibbles, though. When the history of our time is written, Nader will rightfully be a dominating character. He is less about consumerism than the accountability of large institutions. His message is that people count. No one should suppose he's retired. He's still pushing for air bags in cars and new consumer buying groups. He has improved America, and his irritating inquiries still invigorate our democracy. Perpetual perfectibility is an illusion, but thank goodness it's ours.

Newsweek
December 16, 1985

WHY I AM NOT A MANAGER

In 1997, reports the Labor Department, there were 18 million executives, managers, and administrators in the United States. I am not one of them. I have never "managed" anyone or anything. No one works for me or is supervised by me. This is the way it's always been and, almost certainly, will always be. At various employers, no one has ever hinted that I deserved greater power and responsibility. Perish the thought.

All this may explain why I have a certain grudging respect for managers. I am obviously unfit to do whatever it is they do. They seem to relish responsibility, while I dread it. They have, or feign, confidence, while I shudder at putting a subject and verb in every sentence. What also baffles me is why people want to be managers. Granted, some rewards are tempting: power, money, status, and (possibly) the respect of co-workers. But the drawbacks seem as plain: resentment from below; pressure from above; loud criticism of failures; silence over successes. No thanks.

Now, "manager" is a marvelously elastic title. It covers a lot of ground, from exalted CEOs (chief executive officers) to plant managers to school principals—to produce managers at supermarkets. Almost half of all managers (44 percent) are now women, says the Labor Department. In 1997, it counted 711,000 marketing and advertising managers, 535,000 building and real estate managers, 108,000 personnel managers. But along the spectrum of pay and power, many managers face two contradictory demands.

First, they're supposed to get results—to maximize profits, improve test scores, or whatever. Everyone must "perform" these days and be "accountable" (which means being fired, demoted, or chewed out if the desired results aren't forthcoming).

Second, they've got to motivate or manipulate their workers. Gone is the era when machines determined how most work was done. Jobs today are looser. They require initiative or allow leeway. If workers do poorly, the organization suffers. So managers have to command and coddle. They're supposed to be sensitive to workers' problems and "feelings." They should be nice and not nasty. Petty tyrants are disapproved.

The manager mediates between the hard demands of the stock market and the soft demands of workers. On paper, there is no tension. Workers will be committed and creative if they are respected and consulted. Good ideas will bubble up from below. Managers will be rewarded for their openness and understanding. But in real life, conflicts abound. Galvanizing consensus is often time-consuming. Sometimes it's undesirable because some ideas are better than others. And getting people to obey without alienating them is hard if they 1) disagree with you; 2) hate you; 3) are incompetent; or 4) spend the day surfing the Net.

Little wonder, then, that no group in America is more advised and analyzed than managers. I know this, because I receive a steady flow of review copies of management books. Just who reads these books has always puzzled me: if you manage something important, when would you have time? But someone must read them (or at least buy them), because the publishers keep pouring them out. Of course, the publishing industry has a well-deserved reputation for being dim-witted. But it can't be that dim-witted.

Here, for example, are two recent arrivals—*Profit Patterns: 30 Ways to Anticipate and Profit from Strategic Forces Reshaping Your Business* and *The Dance of Change: The Challenges to Sustaining Momentum in Learning Organizations.* As management books go, these seem to be more informative than most. But exactly how will they make it easier for managers to manage?

Profit Patterns reminds us that some companies have clobbered others in head-to-head competition. In 1989, both Apple Computer and Microsoft had stock market capitalizations (the value of all their shares) of about $4 billion. By 1998, Apple was still worth about $4 billion, while Microsoft had zoomed to $220 billion. But Microsoft benefited as much from the blunders of rivals as from its own efforts. IBM let Microsoft keep the licensing rights for the original PC operating software. Big mistake. And Apple didn't license co-production of its computers; this stymied sales and software development.

Companies should spot how "the strategic landscape is changing," says the book. This is a bit abstract. Microsoft's real lesson is simpler: Pray for dumb competitors. If IBM and Apple had been smarter, Bill Gates might be a nobody.

In *The Dance of Change,* we discover that companies often fail at organized efforts of self-improvement. By one study, 70 percent of "reengineering" campaigns founder. Another study estimated that two-thirds of "total quality management" programs do likewise. These failures implicate the capacity of middle managers. Are they guiding change or simply being swept along? "Our core premise," write the authors, "is that the source of these problems cannot be remedied by more expert advice, better consultants or more committed managers." What then follows is 573 pages of musings from experts, consultants, and managers.

The enduring popularity of self-help books like these, I suspect, reflects a widespread insecurity among many managers as a class. (But I also suspect that the best managers disdain these books. They trust their own instincts and knowledge.) The common craving is control; the common fear is chaos. But the latter is rising while the former is falling. Someone must have an answer. In one way or another, all these management books hold out the chimera of control. The fact that they don't deliver may not diminish their appeal: if you're confused, it's reassuring to know that everyone else is, too.

Perhaps managers could once succeed—or at least survive—on status and technical competence. There was a chain of command. Authority was respected or feared. Machines regulated production jobs. This era has ended. The almost universal task of managers today, in our culture, is to serve twin masters, each of whom has grown more demanding. There's the Organization with its imperatives; and there's the Individual—each with "needs." This is a tough job, and somebody's got to do it. But not me.

Newsweek
March 22, 1999

THE INTERNET ISN'T A CHARITY

Capitalism is many things, but charity it isn't. It's about profits, not philanthropy. Here lies the puzzling contradiction of the Internet. It's the jewel of modern capitalism, even though it is now an act of charity. Virtually everything on it (pornography may be an exception) is being given away or sold for less than cost. We know this can't last. Sooner or later the Internet will become profitable. What we don't know is when, how, or with what consequences. The mystery captures the economy's promise—and peril.

It's an old story played before by canals, railroads, and automobiles. Economic and industrial transformations require huge amounts of investment capital. In 1999, new investment in "high technology" (computers, software, communications equipment) rose about 22 percent. All other business investment barely increased at all. The boon of new technologies is that they raise living standards and invent new lifestyles. The bane is that they can spawn overinvestment and competitive carnage. Too many companies crowd the market. Theories of what will work self-destruct. There are booms and busts.

Just about everything that comes over the Internet today loses money. America Online (1999 profits: $762 million) and Yahoo ($61 million) are exceptions. Otherwise, most "content" Web sites—news, financial services, self-help—are free and don't cover costs through advertising. The Internet Advertising Bureau, an industry group, estimates 1999 ad revenues at $4.6 billion, about 2 percent of all ad spending. Competitive Media Reporting, a market research firm, has a lower estimate of on-line ads ($1.9 billion) and says Internet companies spent more ($3.2 billion) advertising themselves in traditional media—TV, newspapers, radio, and magazines.

As for e-retailers, most are gushing red ink. Anthony Noto, an analyst for Goldman Sachs, recently estimated sales and profits for 32 publicly traded e-commerce companies. Only eBay was profitable, and Noto doesn't expect things to change by year-end. Similarly, most business-to-business (B2B) e-commerce projects are too new to be profitable.

Although the Internet is unprofitable, it does generate huge profits for others. The big winners are companies that build the Net by selling computer services, fiber optic cable, "routers," and software. In 1995 Cisco Systems (the leading maker of routers) had sales of $1.98 billion and profits of $421 million. By 1999, sales had passed $12 billion and profits, $2 billion.

The explanation of how profits flow from the unprofitable Internet is this: It's subsidized. Some subsidies come from universities, nonprofit groups, and government. They create Web sites and buy networking equipment. These subsidies may be permanent. But the main subsidies come from capital markets—investors and lenders—and other businesses. In 1999 Internet companies raised almost $18 billion from venture capitalists and another $18 billion from IPOs ("initial public offerings") of stock, reports Thomson Financial Securities Data Corp.

As important, older companies (Wal-Mart, Disney) are spending heavily on Web sites. And communications giants like AT&T are investing lavishly in data networks. All this money covers the gap between the Internet's costs and its revenue. No one knows the size of the gap, but it's certainly large.

Naturally, the subsidies are a bonanza for consumers. Everyone loves something for nothing. After buying computers and paying monthly connect fees, people get the Internet for free. This is surely one reason for its popularity. A survey in March by the Pew Internet & American Life Project found that 90 million Americans have been online. There are still on-line shopping bargains (though they're apparently fading). Amazon.com just sold about 400,000 copies of the latest Harry Potter novel at a 40 percent discount, an admitted loss.

Almost every new venture—big or small—involves start-up costs. Probably no industry has begun without turmoil and temporary losses. In this sense, the Internet is hardly unique. The trouble is that the subsidies won't continue forever. Sooner or later, capital either earns a return or is eliminated by losses. Somehow, commercial Web sites must pay for themselves. If they don't, they will disappear. This is no longer mere theory. Some dot-coms are experiencing scattered layoffs. A few have even vanished.

What's less recognized is that, unless the Internet itself becomes profitable, the companies that build it—the Ciscos, the Oracles—will also suffer. They subsist on today's capital subsidies, which cannot last. The Internet will not continue to expand and thrive unless what it offers becomes self-sustaining. Web services cannot permanently live off subsidies. This means that the costs must somehow be recovered from the people who use it. The joyride for consumers cannot continue indefinitely.

Network television earns its return through national advertising (for consumers, costs are passed along in the price of other products). Cable television and telephones do so through monthly fees. As yet, the Internet has no comparable formula. On paper, there are many possibilities. If the Internet has inherent efficiencies, then some e-retailing, B2B, and other on-line commerce (banking, stock trading, reservations) will flourish. Advertising might support some Web sites with large or loyal audiences. Perhaps companies that provide Internet hookups will also provide customers with some dedicated "content." People would pay for both simultaneously, very much like cable TV. Some other Web sites may become so valuable that users would subscribe—as they don't now—through modest monthly fees.

Who knows? The drama is how and when this inevitable transformation will occur. The Internet cannot coexist forever with its present contradiction. Either the prevailing investment boom will subside, because the capital markets refuse to provide open-ended subsidies. Or ways will be found to make the Internet profitable. Something will ultimately give, because—in the end—the Internet is not a charity.

The Washington Post
July 12, 2000

THE MYSTERIOUS MERGER FRENZY

The most uncovered business story today may be corporate megamergers and, particularly, cross-border mergers. It's not that they've gone unnoticed. Quite the opposite. They've come so rapidly—Daimler-Benz and Chrysler, Exxon and Mobil, Citicorp and Travelers—that they've overwhelmed us. We can't yet gauge their true significance. Perhaps they're spreading technology and lowering costs. Or maybe they're spawning corporate waste and empire-building. They may be creating dangerous concentrations of power—or reviving antitrust regulation. Last week the European Commission killed a venture between Time Warner and British music giant EMI because it might have dominated the recording industry.

We just don't know the larger consequences. By traditional antitrust theory, too many mergers would stifle innovation and raise prices. Yet, the present merger movement coincides with enormous technological change and intensifying competition. This may mean that traditional antitrust theory is flawed. Or it may mean that companies are trying to muffle competition through mergers. Despite the uncertainties, something momentous is clearly happening. The numbers suggest no other conclusion. In 1999 U.S. corporate mergers and acquisitions (M&A) approached $1.5 trillion, according to Mergerstat, a Los Angeles research firm. Since 1994 the cumulative M&A total exceeds $5 trillion. (These figures cover any merger involving a U.S. firm as buyer or seller.)

What's driving the merger explosion? The stated motives run the gamut. There's old-fashioned economies of scale: Buy your competitor in the hope of achieving savings and (perhaps) some market power. This fits the Exxon-Mobil marriage and many others. Then there's the breakdown of old markets: Banks and brokerage houses are merging, because (it's argued) traditional banking and brokerage services are blending into a single service of managing personal and corporate financial needs. And let's not forget technology, which is redefining many major industries. AT&T bought TCI and MediaOne—giant cable firms—because phone, television, and Internet communications are supposedly converging.

Globalization is the last and most interesting merger motive. Once, cross-border mergers were rare. No more. In 1999 they totaled $720 billion, reports a United Nations study. (These numbers cover all global transactions.) Companies are looking for new markets, and governments are more receptive to foreign investment. Between 1991 and 1999, governments made 1,035 major changes affecting foreign investors, says the United Nations. Nine of ten favored more investment. But interestingly, the largest target of the global M&A binge has been the United States. In 1999 foreigners paid $233 billion to buy American companies.

Among many corporations—foreign and American—the urge to expand globally verges on panic. "In a global market, you have to be present everywhere," says Karl Sauvant, director of the U.N. study. "You have to move rapidly [or] your competition will be there first. . . . It's a question of market power, synergies [efficiencies between firms] and spreading risk" among many countries. Sometimes, changing technology impels companies to go global. Deutsche Telekom, the German phone company, proposes to buy VoiceStream, a second-tier U.S. wireless firm, to gain a toehold in the American market. The theory is that, in wireless technology, only firms with worldwide reach and size will ultimately survive.

The theory sounds sensible. It might even be right. But every past merger wave has had its theories, and many were wrong. Big mergers often flop, according to much academic scholarship. They don't raise profits or lower costs. Claimed efficiencies never materialize. The practical and human problems of melding two large enterprises prove crippling. These past failures haven't much deterred today's executives. "It's like marriage," says Sauvant. "You know that 50 percent fail, but you don't think it will be you."

Corporate judgments may not have improved. Consider the 1998 Daimler-Chrysler merger. The main architects were Daimler's chairman Jurgen Schrempp and the then Chrysler chairman Robert Eaton. "Eaton lusted after Daimler's quality and engineering. Schrempp coveted Chrysler's gutsy attitude and quick reactions," write Bill Vlasic and Bradley Stertz in their superb book, *Taken for a Ride: How Daimler-Benz Drove Off with Chrysler.* Savings would be massive, $1.4 billion in the first year alone.

Perhaps the dream will one day be realized; it hasn't yet. Overall profitability is declining, even though the company says it achieved first-year savings. In the third quarter, Chrysler announced its first operating loss ($530 million) since the third quarter of 1991. Although portrayed as a union of equals, the merger was a takeover by Daimler-Benz. Personal and cultural conflicts abounded, as Vlasic and Stertz show. The company's stock has plunged. After the merger, it opened at about $75 and rose to $108 in early 1999. It's now trading at about $44 or $45. The market value of the combined company roughly equals Daimler-Benz's value alone before the merger.

What's intriguing is that the surge in foreign investment hasn't yet stirred much nationalistic backlash. In this current economic boom, perhaps no one worries about anything. Or people may recall that the loud fears about Japanese investment a decade ago proved largely foundless. In all, foreigners control less than 10 percent of U.S. business.

For the moment the pressing question is whether all the mergers make economic sense. Because every merger is unique, generalizations are hazardous. Still, the question lingers, and there are two broad theories. One is that the mergers invigorate the economy. They shake things up, advance new technologies, and improve profitability. They sustain the boom. The other theory is that the mergers are a by-product of the boom. High stock prices and fat profits have sent executives prowling for acquisitions which—because they are fed more by ambition than logic—will ultimately undermine profits, stock prices, and the boom. Good times breed their own undoing. Sobering thought.

Newsweek
October 16, 2000

PART V

WELFARE

WHAT MONEY CAN'T BUY

Everyone involved in "welfare reform" could usefully read *What Money Can't Buy* (Harvard University Press), a study by sociologist Susan Mayer of the University of Chicago. Its message is somber: As a society, we are fairly helpless to correct the worst problems of child poverty. This is not a new insight, but by confirming it, Mayer discredits much of the welfare debate's overwrought rhetoric. "Welfare reform" may raise or lower poverty a bit (we can't say which), but neither its supposed virtues nor its alleged vices are powerful enough to alter the status quo dramatically.

What's impressive about Mayer's study is that it contradicts both her politics and her history. She's a registered Democrat, a self-described "hard-nosed" liberal. She does not write explicitly about welfare but instead asks a basic question: How important is money in enabling families to help their children escape poverty? Having once been a single mother without much money, she believed that money was critical. "It's terrible to be a parent," she says, "and not be able to buy things that your kids want." She recalls having to borrow to pay a doctor's bill. Money must matter. Well, it doesn't—at least, not much.

Mayer reviewed studies and tried to match parents' incomes with children's outcomes. Good outcomes were high test scores, having a job (or being in school) at the age of 24, and earning high wages. Bad outcomes included dropping out of high school and becoming an unwed mother. Of course, children of middle-class parents do better than children of poorer parents. Mayer tried to distinguish between the pure income effects and other influences. Once she does, income's impact drops sharply. (Warning to potential readers: A lot of the book is technical.) She writes:

"The parental characteristics that employers value and are willing to pay for, such as skills, diligence, honesty, good health, and reliability, also improve children's life chances, independent of their effect on parents' incomes. Children of parents with these attributes do well even if their parents do not have much income." This demolishes much of the welfare debate's rhetorical boilerplate, liberal and conservative.

As Mayer notes, it "flies in the face of the common liberal claim that 'the poor are just like everyone else except that they have less money.' " Indeed, the material well-being of poor children has generally improved, report Mayer and sociologist Christopher Jencks of Harvard in another study. In 1970, about 26 percent of the poorest fifth of children hadn't visited a doctor in the past year; by 1989, the figure was only 14 percent. In 1973, about 71 percent of these children lived in homes without air-conditioning; by 1991, only 45 percent did. Unfortunately, these material improvements didn't translate into better social conditions. Crime rose; so did out-of-wedlock birthrates.

But Mayer's study also shakes the reassuring conservative assumption that, if pushed, the poor can become self-sufficient through work. Precisely because many long-term welfare recipients aren't as competent or disciplined as middle-class parents, they may not find and keep jobs, let alone well-paying ones. The thrust of Mayer's grim analysis is to support the existence of a permanent "culture of poverty," an argument first advanced in the modern American context by political scientist Edward Banfield in a 1970 book.

Banfield split the poor into two groups. Some simply lacked money. These included many disabled and unemployed people and some single mothers, who had been widowed, divorced, or abandoned. These people had middle-class values and could benefit from government income support. They could usually recover from a setback (job loss, divorce). Then there was the true "lower class," who would "live in squalor . . . even if their incomes were doubled," Banfield wrote, because they had a "radically present-oriented" outlook that "attaches no value to work, sacrifice, self-improvement, or service to family, friends or community."

The Banfield theory ignited outrage, because it meant that, beyond some point, the effort to end poverty would fail. In the prevailing climate—all problems were then deemed solvable—this was heresy. But it has stood the test of time and taps into popular ambivalence about social welfare. For 200 years Americans "have vacillated between trying to improve the material well-being of poor children and . . . the moral character of their parents," says Mayer.

Early in the nineteenth century, localities provided the poor with "outdoor relief" (a handout of money, food, or goods). Later, the poor were shunted into almshouses, intended to promote work, temperance, and character.

The present "welfare reform" fits this tradition. It is not as harsh as critics charge. (The one exception is the cutoff in benefits to legal immigrants; but this involves immigration, another matter.) For example, it does not impose an absolute five-year lifetime welfare limit (a fifth of a state's caseload can exceed five years). It correctly presumes that what people do for themselves matters more than what government does for them. By allowing states to experiment with mixes of benefits and work requirements, we may discover which policies succeed.

But reform could easily fail. The real test is not reduced welfare caseloads. These have already dropped 21 percent since early 1994, mainly as the result of a strong economy. The real tests are less teenage pregnancy, more stable marriages, and better homes for children. It's a tall order—perhaps an impossible one—for government to reengineer family life and human nature. And, of course, not all poor families are on welfare.

The dilemma is to maintain an adequate safety net without being so generous as to create more dependency. Mayer doubts that expanding the safety net would do much good. It now meets most families' basic needs—one reason, she suspects, why extra income doesn't much improve children's prospects. But she fears that scaling assistance back sharply might do harm. Still, she has no pat solutions. After finishing her study, she felt depressed by the realization that ending poverty "may be beyond the capacity of even a rich nation."

Newsweek
May 5, 1997

MYTH OF THE MANAGED
CARE MONSTER

If my wife or children become sick, I want the best possible medical care for them. I might even like the same for myself. We all would. But if all of us can get whatever health care we—or our doctors—want, then society will ultimately be worse off. Growing health costs will progressively prevent us from spending much more on anything else. This is the dilemma of a nation obsessed with individual well-being that must, somehow, also protect its collective well-being. We barely acknowledge it.

The latest health debate involves the patients' "bill of rights," a phrase adopted by both Democrats and Republicans. The common language is significant. It panders (as politicians love to do) to the popular belief that we can avoid messy ethical, political, and economic choices simply by legislating an appealing list of patients' "rights." It isn't that easy. Unless someone can say no to health spending that might be futile, unnecessary, or self-indulgent, costs will spin out of control.

If boundaries between wise and unwise treatment were always clear, there would be little controversy or confusion. But typically,

they aren't. What may seem hopeless surgery to some distant analyst may seem—if it's my son or mother—imperative to me. There's
an unavoidable collision between our personal instincts and society's wider interest in ensuring that health spending significantly
improves people's health. Anyone playing "gatekeeper" (that is,
making the decisions) courts unpopularity.

In recent years, the job has fallen increasingly to "managed care."
The patients' "bill of rights" reflects an alleged backlash against
this. We've all heard the stories: emergency room coverage denied
because advance approval wasn't obtained; patients barred from
specialists they—or their doctors—want; people hustled out of hospitals while they still seem sick. Managed care often seems pitiless,
capricious, and incompetent. Sometimes the stigma is deserved; as
often, it's exaggerated.

People imagine the worst from managed care; they usually don't
experience it. Most Americans rate their health care favorably: 66
percent of those in managed care compared to 76 percent in "fee for
service" medicine, finds a survey for the Kaiser Family Foundation.
(Under fee for service, doctors and hospitals set their fees and are
typically reimbursed by insurers. Managed care uses salaried doctors
or negotiates lower fees.) The Kaiser survey documents fears that
coverage might be denied but also finds that the fears reflect "rare
events that seem threatening," reports the journal *Health Affairs.*

It's also a myth that the main obstacle to good care is some callous managed care accountant. Studies may someday show that
managed care has pervasively lowered quality. For now, though, the
more common threats arise from mistakes and sloppy practices by
nurses, doctors, and hospitals. A presidential commission on health
care quality found widespread "overutilization of services, under-
utilization of services, and errors." All these problems predate managed care's huge expansion in the 1990s.

One 1988 study of deaths from stroke, pneumonia, and heart
attack in 12 hospitals "indicated that 14 percent could have been
prevented [with] adequate diagnosis and treatment," said the commission. A review of Medicare patients—most under "fee for ser-

vice"—found that only 21 percent of heart attack victims "received beta blockers within 90 days" of an attack, although "those receiving beta blockers had a 43 percent lower rate of mortality."

Just because doctors, in good conscience, recommend a given treatment doesn't mean it's always needed. John Wennberg of Dartmouth Medical School and his associates have shown in many studies that patients with similar conditions often receive different treatments—some far more costly than others—with little difference in results. The promise of managed care is to promote the "best practices" by emphasizing what's effective and eliminating what's not; the danger is that, under the guise of doing this, it will deny or delay sensible care.

The patients' "rights" debate skirts these practical problems and instead treats managed care as an all-purpose ogre that is defeating the promise of modern medicine. To do otherwise would be to admit that managed care is an instrument of rationing—a process whose existence Americans deny, even though it is inevitable. Lost in all the rhetoric are two important realities.

First, the backlash against managed care is most powerful among doctors, not patients. It is doctors whose independence and incomes are most threatened. Their decisions are reviewed and sometimes reversed. They face maddening rules and reimbursement practices. In negotiations, their fees are squeezed. Between 1992 and 1994, doctors' average incomes stagnated at $182,000, though they later rose to $199,000 in 1996.

Second, managed care has (at least temporarily) controlled health costs. Between 1965 and 1990, health spending rose about 11 percent annually. It grew from 5.7 percent of national income (gross domestic product) to 12.2 percent. The increases defied government and voluntary controls. One reason is that doctors and hospitals had an economic interest to order as much care as possible. But since 1995, increases have averaged 3 to 4 percent. Subdued health costs have helped lower inflation and raise wages.

All this suggests caution in new legislation. Some standards are needed, because some managed care groups are worse than others.

There should be quick appeals from adverse coverage decisions. "Prudent" use of emergency rooms should be protected. But more sweeping proposals—embodied mainly in Democratic plans—could cripple cost control. They contain many provisions that would curb the power of managed care groups to oversee doctors and hospitals. These might improve doctors' incomes more than patients' health. The Congressional Budget Office says this legislation could ultimately raise health premiums 4 percent.

Whatever happens—whether some proposal becomes law or not—patients' "rights" will remain elusive. It's a clever phrase that obscures larger social choices. Medicine is the most personal of services; yet its promise makes it ever more technological, bureaucratic, and costly. The dilemmas ensure many deceptive debates and disappointing "reforms."

The Washington Post
July 29, 1998

POISONOUS SYMBOLISM

Our politics increasingly subsist on symbolism. We argue furiously over policies that purport to advance "family values" or to suppress obscenity or to honor some group, when these policies—whether adopted or not—wouldn't affect most intended beneficiaries. These poisonous debates mainly encourage political breast-beating; each side flaunts its own moral superiority. Nowhere is this truer than in matters of race and ethnicity and, in particular, in affirmative action. Indeed, the debate on affirmative action is now almost completely disconnected from the facts.

The antagonists are so self-righteous that they have embraced the common assumption that these programs are important—for good or ill, depending on one's view—to ordinary Americans. This must be so for advocates to claim that affirmative action is an essential remedy for racial, ethnic, or sexual injustice. And it must be so if critics are to decry affirmative action as widespread reverse discrimination. But it isn't so. Affirmative action programs don't matter much for most Americans.

By affirmative action, I do not mean "outreach" programs in college or job recruiting. Nor do I mean a general consciousness of race, sex, or ethnicity that causes companies or colleges—when judging people of similar merit—to strive for some racial or sexual balance. These mild forms of affirmative action stir little controversy. The disagreement centers on programs that may slide into preferences or quotas. That's what President Clinton defends, as he did again last week at the NAACP's annual convention, and that's where studies typically find small effects. Consider:

• *College admissions:* Preferences are used only by elite schools (those whose students have SAT scores in the top 20 percent), report economists Thomas Kane of Harvard and William Dickens of the Brookings Institution. Ending preferences would "have little impact" on who goes to college, because almost everyone could get into other schools (admission rates exceed 90 percent). The main effect would be to shuffle spots at elite colleges.

• *Jobs:* The affirmative action programs required of companies with federal contracts seem to raise black employment only slightly and to lower Hispanic employment, conclude economists William Rodgers III of William and Mary and William Spriggs of the Commerce Department. In 1992, blacks were 13 percent of the workers for federal contractors, compared with 11.7 percent of workers in the labor force. Hispanics constituted 7.1 percent of workers at contractors, lower than their 7.6 percent share of the labor force. (Rodgers and Spriggs can't explain the difference.)

• *Government procurement:* Set-aside programs do little to foster minority-owned businesses. In the late 1980s, only about 12 percent of minority firms had sales to state or local governments, and two-thirds of these relied on government for less than 25 percent of their sales, say economists Timothy Bates and Darrell Williams of Wayne State University. But firms that depend heavily on government (25 percent or more of sales) actually have a much higher failure rate. They're vulnerable to contract loss.

The major gains for blacks and women have flowed from antidiscrimination laws and a shift in social attitudes, not affirmative action. Similarly, the great remaining problems for blacks—family breakdown, inadequate workplace skills—defy solution by affirmative action. But the debate proceeds as if these programs have immense significance. The scholars who show otherwise are not necessarily diehard critics. Often, the opposite. Harvard's Kane endorses preferences at elite colleges. It's important, he says, to have diverse student bodies at schools that produce society's leaders. Similarly, Rodgers and Spriggs support federal affirmative action job requirements.

In light of the research, the case is hard to make. I have no doubt that these programs do some good for some people. Kane's study finds that after controlling for the usual factors (family income, etc.), blacks from elite colleges enjoy a payoff—in terms of higher salaries—similar to whites'. Abolishing preferences would hurt some; black acceptances slumped at UC Berkeley's law school when preferences ended. But the benefits of these programs no longer justify the social costs.

What's sacrificed is a basic principle—that people should be judged as individuals and not on the basis of race or sex—for gains to a few people. Affirmative action also sends a hurtful message to blacks and other favored groups. Shelby Steele's 1990 book, *The Content of Our Character,* put this eloquently:

"Blacks cannot be repaid for the injustice done to the race, but we can be corrupted by society's guilty gestures of repayment. Affirmative action is such a gesture. It tells us that racial preferences can do for us what we cannot do for ourselves. . . . This is an incentive to be reliant on others just as we are struggling for self-reliance." And people who succeed on their own risk having their achievement stigmatized as an artifact of affirmative action.

Finally, affirmative action sows racial, ethnic, and sexual ill will. Whites may blame setbacks (over college or jobs) on those who benefit from preferences. But the resentment is overblown, as Kane and Dickens show. Consider Harvard, they say. It has 18,000 applicants for 1,600 spots each year. About 90 percent will be disappointed. Now consider that about 15 percent of Harvard students (about 240) are black or Hispanic. Even if all benefited from preferences—clearly not the case—ending preferences would help only 240 more white students. Still, many whites "may falsely believe they would be accepted" but for preferences.

I doubt that affirmative action programs would survive a genuine appreciation of their limited benefits. Actually, affirmative action programs probably won't survive anyway, because as political scientist George La Noue of the University of Maryland reminds us, courts are slowly disallowing preferences except as a remedy for proven discrimination. And California voters rejected preferences in Proposition 209. The dismantling will be needlessly wrenching if we continue to focus more on symbolism than on facts.

Newsweek
July 28, 1997

REINVENTING RETIREMENT

John Glenn's return to space has captivated most of us and awed a few of us. Although it may be mainly a publicity stunt, it surely exemplifies the new truism that old age isn't what it used to be. We won't learn much about the body from Glenn's experiments, but the fact that a 77-year-old man is now orbiting the globe is a vivid reminder of the debate we're not having on earth. This, of course, involves America's inevitable aging.

Our policies toward the elderly rest on outdated assumptions. When Congress created Social Security in 1935, life expectancy was 62 years, and the 65-and-over population was tiny. At Medicare's birth in 1965, life expectancy was 70 years. The assumptions were that the elderly, defined as anyone 65 and over, were automatically decrepit and dependent. The decent thing (it was thought) was to protect them against impoverishment.

But the underlying assumptions no longer hold. Life expectancy is now 76—and climbing. Glenn's exploit is exceptional only for its visibility. We read every day of older Americans doing things that are more exacting: running marathons, climbing mountains. People

not only live longer, they are healthier. The infirmities that ultimately afflict us all either occur later or are more treatable than ever.
Yet age 65 still survives in politics and popular culture as the threshold of "elderly."

In popular culture, it is bound to crumble. Feats like Glenn's has-
ten the process. As older members of the baby boom approach 60
(they are now in their early fifties), they will insist on their own vitality and relevance. They will invent new labels—some, no doubt,
absurd and pretentious—for their latest life stage. But in politics,
change is less certain, though no less necessary.

A recent report by the Congressional Budget Office (CBO),
"Long-term Budgetary Pressures and Policy Options," shows why.
In 1997, Social Security cost 4 percent of national income (gross
domestic product, or GDP), Medicare 3 percent, and Medicaid 1
percent. (Medicare is federal health insurance for the elderly; Medicaid covers much nursing home care.) That's 8 percent of GDP.
Under present policies, CBO projects that to rise to 13 percent of
GDP by 2020, a 63 percent increase. Social Security hits 6 percent
of GDP, Medicare 5 percent, and Medicaid 2 percent.

There are only a few ways to cope: pay for the higher benefits by
raising taxes; lower other spending; run big budget deficits; or reduce the benefits by making programs less generous. In practice, we
may do all four. But the hardest—and most essential—is to reduce
future benefits.

We need to redraft the generational compact. Social Security,
Medicare, and Medicaid are pay-as-you-go programs. Workers support retirees. According to the CBO, the average person between 65
and 79 receives $12,000 in federal benefits (mainly Social Security
and Medicare) and pays $4,800 in taxes; meanwhile, the average
person between 20 and 64 pays $8,100 in taxes and receives $1,500
in direct federal benefits. To pay future benefits entirely by taxes
would mean huge increases for workers.

This is neither defensible nor desirable. These immense intergen-
erational transfers require some justification, and the truth is that the
moral claims of the old on the young—through government pro-

grams—have lost much of their original power. Two arguments are standard.

First, the old cannot cope for themselves; therefore, a caring society tries to ensure them some minimum standard of living. This may still be true, but it is no longer true at age 65 and surely not at age 62 (when the average person leaves the labor force).

Second, the old could not plan for their retirements because they did not know how long they would live. This was more true in the 1950s and 1960s—when life expectancy rose unexpectedly—than today. A prudent person now plans for a long retirement. This argument applies only to those who live much longer than average.

Return now to Glenn. Since his ascent, we've heard much gushy rhetoric about making better use of the "talents and energy of the elderly." Well, the best use of their talents would be to have more of them work longer. They need to pay for more of their own retirements. Put crudely, they need not become a social burden at a relatively tender age.

In practice, early retirement has to become harder. Social Security's eligibility age needs to be raised (the age for full benefits is now scheduled to reach 67 by the year 2027; it should go higher, probably to 70, and faster). The elderly should pay more of Medicare's costs through higher premiums and co-payments. And tax breaks for those over 65—including exempting part of Social Security from income taxes—should be repealed. So should Social Security's earnings test, which penalizes people for working by reducing their benefits.

All this may seem harsh, even "anti-elderly." It isn't. I'm not suggesting that everyone work 60 hours a week until age 90. As people grow older, they may want to mix work and leisure through part-time, part-year, or intermittent jobs. The U.S. economy excels at creating new types of jobs to fit people's social needs. And the economy will need more workers, because an aging America will have a small labor pool. In 1997, there were almost five Americans between 20 and 64 for every American 65 and over; by 2030, that ratio is projected to fall below three to one.

Nor am I arguing that changes in taxes and benefits be made abruptly. They should be phased in to give people ample warning. I am 52. Changes would apply mainly to the baby boom generation. They would prevent us from overtaxing our children. The longer changes are delayed, the harder they'll be and the more conflict we'll have. But delay is what we've done, in part because today's elderly resist any changes and politicians pander to them.

We need to reinvent retirement. This is not an accounting exercise. It should reflect a sense of collective responsibility and present social realities. Glenn's space voyage shows how those realities have altered. Our programs for the elderly support more and more people who are more and more independent for longer and longer periods. What started as a sensible concern for the old is evolving into a selfish plundering of the young.

The Washington Post
November 4, 1998

RACISM AND POVERTY

"A Common Destiny: Blacks and American Society"—a massive study released last week by the National Research Council—isn't pleasant reading. It took dozens of scholars four years to complete and is intended to update two earlier reports ("An American Dilemma" by Swedish economist Gunnar Myrdal in 1944 and the Kerner commission report in 1968). There's lots of good news about how race relations have improved since the 1940s. But the basic message is dispiriting: Our race problem today is so stubborn because poverty, not discrimination, is its main cause.

Some of the good news bears repeating, because many younger Americans don't know much of the gruesome past. In 1940, 77 percent of blacks lived in the South under forced segregation. By law, they were required to drink from separate fountains and attend separate schools. Informal segregation was also pervasive. In this age of Michael Jordan, can anyone believe that blacks came to the National Basketball Association only in 1950? Until World War II, three-quarters of the few black college graduates went into two segregated professions, the clergy and teaching.

Outlawing legal segregation allowed many blacks to enter the mainstream. President Reagan's last national security adviser was black. In 1940, there were 300 black engineers; by 1980, there were 36,019. The black middle class has expanded. The share of black families with annual incomes above $35,000 (adjusted for inflation) was 13.1 percent in 1967, 20.9 percent in 1979, and 22.3 percent in 1987. But this progress has not erased black poverty. Between 1967 and 1987, the share of families with incomes under $10,000 rose from 28.3 to 30 percent.

Suppose someone had a plan—training programs, child care, or whatever—to make all the working-age poor (blacks, whites, and others) productive and self-supporting. Suppose the plan cost $100 billion annually, but success was guaranteed in 20 years. My hunch is that most Americans would support it. We don't like poverty. It's a source of national shame. It encourages crime. Yet nothing like this is on the public agenda. The main reason, I think, is not stinginess or indifference. It's skepticism.

People doubt government's power to create such a transformation, and without good prospects of success, they won't gamble vast amounts. Looking just at blacks, we know the main explanation for the widening gap between the middle class and poor. It's family breakdown. Half of all black families with children under 18 are headed by women, up from a quarter in 1960. Half of black children live in these female-headed families; two-thirds of these children are (by the government's definition) in poverty.

Theories abound why many black men abandon their children. Welfare (it's said) gives women an alternative and relieves men of responsibility. Although "Blacks and American Society" belittles this idea, there's probably something to it. Black men often can't provide for families even if they do stick around; their employment rates have fallen, and their crime rates have risen. Since 1970, many low-skilled but good-paying jobs have vanished and wage growth has slowed. In 1972, almost three-quarters of black men over 20 were employed; the share now is two-thirds.

Short of an economic miracle, there are no easy ways to make heroic gains against these trends. By themselves, more schooling and more social services are no answer. (Indeed, black poverty has persisted despite gains in school attendance. The average black today is a high school graduate; in 1960, most had finished only junior high.) People become self-supporting and productive mainly through their own efforts. What government can do is help those who help themselves. To aid all the poor (not just blacks), we should

• *reward work.* The working poor should keep all they make in the market. This means offsetting the taxes they pay—mainly Social Security and sales taxes—through a more generous earned-income tax credit. Congress is moving in this direction. But the size and coverage of tax relief should be expanded greatly. Now, only workers with children (including single parents) qualify. Coverage should also go to single workers and poor, childless couples.

• *emphasize education.* What matters is education, not schooling. Degrees that don't reflect real skills and knowledge are worthless. Strict competency tests for high school diplomas and teaching jobs are critical. Without pressures for higher standards, more money for schools will be wasted. Lowering standards to prevent dropouts may raise attendance rates but won't improve students' prospects.

• *get serious about crime.* Blacks are the most frequent victims of black crime. For the young, crime discourages work and undermines schools because it's so profitable. It feeds drug use—which promotes more crime—and terrorizes neighborhoods. Getting serious about crime means more police, more prosecutors, and more prisons.

The trouble with these simple ideas is that they cost money (though not that much in a $5-trillion economy) and will at best produce only gradual gains. But doing nothing is more dangerous. The menacing connection between economics and emotion is this: Poverty breeds racism. As "Blacks and American Society" shows, there are still vast gaps in attitudes between blacks and whites. Many whites think racism and discrimination are things of the past, while many blacks blame whites for holding them down.

There's much hypocrisy (among whites) and self-delusion (among blacks) in these attitudes. Yes, whites support racial equality in opinion polls. But many whites shun neighborhoods with large numbers of blacks. So housing segregation remains widespread. Meanwhile, blacks delude themselves by thinking that their problems would recede if only whites cared more and tried harder. Affirmative action, for example, won't cure black poverty. It won't turn unskilled blacks into computer programmers.

A society in which blacks and whites don't have similar life opportunities belies the American dream. Given that, poverty and racism are almost bound to feed on each other. As long as black poverty stays high, many whites will assume that all blacks are like poor blacks. And many blacks will continue to think in group terms, holding whites responsible for all black ills. It's this connection that makes our race problem so disheartening.

Newsweek
August 7, 1989

DILEMMAS OF DISABILITY

Nearly a decade after its creation, the Americans with Disabilities Act (ADA) of 1990 is a case study in the limits of social engineering. Last week the Supreme Court either gutted the ADA or imbued it with common sense—depending on your point of view. The court ruled that people with common problems (eyesight that requires glasses, for example) aren't "disabled" under the law. But even if the court had gone the other way, it couldn't have rewritten the ADA's record of underwhelming achievement.

The ADA aimed to bring the most disabled Americans into the mainstream by getting them jobs. Work (the logic went) would increase income, limit dependence, and raise self-respect. So the ADA outlawed job discrimination against the disabled and required employers to provide "reasonable accommodations" for otherwise qualified workers. Despite these protections, the ADA has raised the employment of the most disabled only slightly.

The Census Bureau says that about 9 percent of the working-age population (those 20 to 64) are "severely disabled"—meaning, generally, that they use a wheelchair or cane, have serious hearing or sight problems, or are mentally retarded. Among them, employment rose from 23 percent to 26 percent between 1991 and 1994. A private poll by the Harris Survey in 1998 suggests a similar job level. Conceivably, the increase (800,000 individuals between 1991 and 1994) could stem from the ADA. But it could also reflect the economic recovery.

This does not mean the ADA has utterly failed. John Lancaster, executive director of the President's Committee on Employment of People with Disabilities, puts it this way: "The ADA [has altered] attitudes about people with disabilities: what they can and can't do. . . . They're able to get around better. You see more [disabled] people out there. The attitudinal things break down when you see people as people and not as wheelchairs."

Point taken. The ADA also has made the public landscape friendlier for the disabled. Businesses and governments had to make themselves more accessible. Doors were widened, curb sides lowered, toilet stalls enlarged, ramps installed, and parking spaces reserved. A lot of this was uneconomical. (The commuter buses I ride were fitted with wheelchair elevators; I have seen them used only once.) But the changes not only helped the disabled, they also signaled a larger social acceptance.

Still, the employment effect is weak. Why?

Laws can do only so much. Even before the ADA, many severely disabled people worked. Character and circumstances count. My best friend, a newspaper editor, developed Parkinson's disease a decade ago. He never thought of quitting, and even without the ADA, I doubt his paper would have fired him. He's too competent and conscientious. But the ADA rendered the issue moot by requiring employers to make "reasonable accommodations."

The costs of doing so are probably not high. In about 70 percent of cases, companies' expenses are less than $500, says the President's Committee. What's false is the accompanying assumption that the disabled lack jobs mainly because employers are indifferent, ignorant, or hostile. The messier truth is that some disabled can't work—and some don't want to. What to do?

Well, provide a safety net. In 1998, Social Security's disability program had 6.3 million beneficiaries and cost $48 billion; the Supplemental Security Income program had 5.3 million disability beneficiaries and cost $24 billion. Most also got government health insurance, Medicare, or Medicaid.

Here lies the great contradiction. The ADA wants the disabled to work. But if you pay people for being disabled, more will say they're disabled and won't work. This is especially true of people with low skills, whose job prospects and potential wages are poorest. Among "severely disabled" college graduates, half worked in 1994. Among high school graduates, less than a third did. The easiest way to increase work among the disabled would be to reduce disability benefits or raise eligibility requirements.

This isn't likely. It would seem heartless. Indeed, the term *disabled* has grown looser over time. Many advocates who want the disabled in the mainstream also want more people considered disabled. They see little conflict between demanding that the disabled be treated like everyone else, while insisting that more physical and mental problems be labeled disabilities, entitling people to special treatment.

In the 1980s, Social Security tried to hold down disability costs by tightening eligibility. The effort collapsed after a political outcry and adverse court rulings. As a result, Social Security's disability rolls include people who can't work (a fourth die within five years)—and many who could. The White House would cope with the dilemma by allowing many disabled to keep government benefits while working. The Senate passed a bill to permit up to six years of Medicare coverage for beneficiaries who work. This skirts the hard political, administrative, and moral problems of critically inspecting who's disabled.

A similar dilemma afflicts the ADA. The broader the definition of "disabled," the more the law becomes a tool for the already employed to raise their pay. In one case before the Supreme Court, two pilots at regional airlines applied for better jobs at United, which rejected them because their uncorrected vision fell below the company's standard. In another case, an auto mechanic was fired because his job involved driving trucks and his blood pressure exceeded the company's requirement. He got another job. The court ruled these workers weren't disabled.

That's common sense—but perhaps not congressional intent. When it passed the ADA, Congress didn't strictly define "disability." The law exudes grand ambitions and vague language. To be precise would have highlighted the central dilemma: The problems of the seriously disabled aren't easily solved; and the problems of the mildly disabled aren't very serious.

The Washington Post
June 30, 1999

THE TYPICAL HOUSEHOLD ISN'T

We ought to retire the "median household income" as a major indicator of social well-being, because it no longer means what most people think it means. By the official figures (the 1996 estimate was released last week), the typical American household has about the same income now as in 1970. Consider. In 1996, median household income—the income at the middle of the income distribution—was $35,492. In 1970, it was $33,181. That's a rise of 7 percent over 26 years. Not much. (Both figures are in 1996 "inflation adjusted" dollars.) Actually, most Americans have experienced slow but significant income gains over this period.

How could it be otherwise?

Since the early 1970s, the economy has spread many new consumer goods and services throughout the population: personal computers (and now the Internet), artificial hips, video games, call waiting, microwave ovens. People eat out more often; they fly more often; homes have gotten bigger. You can debate the value of these new conveniences and customs, but you can't argue that they're free. They all cost money; so, the idea that typical incomes have stagnated seems absurd. And it is. The statistics aren't lying, but they've been widely misinterpreted.

A central problem is that the household in the middle isn't typical anymore. For years, the median-income household has been regarded as the ordinary household. In our mind's eye, it was a married couple with one or two children. In the 1950s or 1960s, the image wasn't wildly inaccurate. There was more uniformity. But today, Americans marry later, divorce more often, live longer, and have more children out of wedlock.

The result is that since the early 1970s, there has been a surge in households—singles, childless couples, single-parent families— that don't fit the conventional image of "typical." Everyone knows this, but that hasn't altered how we view the income statistics. It should. If two people earning $20,000 each divorce, the result is two households of $20,000 instead of one with $40,000. A couple that ages from 60 to 75 may see its income (after peak work years) slip from $50,000 to $35,000: lower, but still adequate. Single parents typically have lower incomes.

All these changes depress median household income. Looking at the figures another way produces a much different picture of income changes. Instead of examining all households together, study them by their size. What's happened to the incomes of singles (households with one person) or households with two, three, or four people? The answer is that incomes have consistently risen over long periods. Here, for example, is the story for singles. (The figures reflect the median—the midpoint—for singles and, again, are in 1996 dollars. All these statistics are available at a special Census Bureau Web site: http://www.census.gov/hhes/www/income.html)

1970: $11,792
1980: $15,560
1989: $18,763 (peak)
1996: $17,897

The gain between 1970 and 1996 is almost 52 percent; since

1980, it's 15 percent. By these numbers, there has been a small drop since the peak year of 1989.

Look now at households with four people. The pattern of the median is similar, though less dramatic.

1970: $42,458
1980: $46,536
1989: $51,554 (peak)
1996: $51,405

The gain since 1970 is 21 percent; since 1980, it's about 10.5 percent. The same pattern also holds for households with two people and three people, though actual numbers differ slightly. (It's not true for households with six people and seven or more, but these households represent only about 3 percent of the total. For five-person households—about 7 percent of the total—incomes are up slightly since 1970.) Still, even these figures show no gains since the late 1980s. Could that be true?

It might, though stagnation seems at odds with a strong economy. But here, too, there's cause for suspicion. In the early 1990s, the Census Bureau (which compiles the figures) made some technical changes that may have reduced reported incomes. And recall that the consumer price index probably overstates inflation because it doesn't fully measure the improvements in new products or consumers' tendency to shop for the best buys (by, say, going to discounters). If inflation is overstated, then true income is understated. Some economists put the error at 1 percent or more a year; but even at half that (0.5 percent), incomes would be noticeably higher than in the official figures.

But the larger point is that America has changed so much that median household income no longer reflects the changing economic status of the mythical middle-income family. What reinforces this conclusion is another upheaval since the late 1960s: surging immigration. It, too, depresses median incomes.

Many immigrants are low skilled. They may be richer here than in their country of birth, but their average incomes are below those of native-born Americans. That's also true of many Americans born of immigrants. Immigration is one reason that the poverty rate (13.7 percent in 1996) has stayed high. Since 1972, more than half the rise in poverty has occurred among Hispanics. Since 1989, the effect is larger. Hispanics account for two-thirds of the increase in poverty. Asian Americans account for another 10 percent. (By contrast, the poverty rate among blacks has dropped. In 1996, it was 28.4 percent. Though still appallingly high, that was the lowest on record.)

The misuse of the median income endures mainly out of habit and laziness. Many analysts and reporters simply do what they've always done. But some advocates on the Left and Right deliberately misuse it. They want to portray incomes as stagnating to bolster the case for their pet economic agendas. Properly interpreted, though, incomes aren't stagnating. The real message from the numbers is that our major problems are not economic but social (an aging society, family breakdown, immigration, a culture of poverty). And these are problems for which we have no quick fixes.

The Washington Post
October 8, 1997

THE TWO-EARNER MYTH

Few ideas are so deeply embedded in popular consciousness and political debate as what I'll call the "two-earner myth." It holds that two workers—a husband and a wife—are now needed to make the same income that one worker—the husband—attained in the 1950s and 1960s. Women have flooded into the labor market (the theory holds) mostly to offset the lost earnings of their husbands. Her income restores the couple's living standards to where they would have been if his wages weren't dropping. Families feel stressed. And why not? Mothers must choose between putting food on the table and caring for their children.

The theory has broad appeal. Conservatives see it as one reason that "traditional" families are under assault; liberals view it as a pretext for aggressive government programs to raise economic growth. But the theory is mostly bogus, though not the feelings that go with it (as I will explain in a moment). Here's what actually has happened:

• *Women didn't initially enter the job market to make up losses in their husbands' salaries.* The influx began in the 1950s, two decades before any slowdown in men's wages. Between 1950 and 1970, the proportion of wives with paid jobs rose from 23 to 39 percent. By 1995, it was 61 percent. Maybe the pioneer working wives of the 1950s and 1960s sought to raise their families' incomes; if so, the reason wasn't their husbands' falling wages. Most wages rose rapidly during these decades.

• *Since the early 1970s, men's wage growth has slowed.* But the increase in the number of wives with jobs is concentrated among upper-income couples—precisely those who need the extra money least. Among the richest fifth of husbands, the share of working wives rose from 45 to 71 percent between 1973 and 1993, reports economist Gary Burtless of the Brookings Institution. Wealthier husbands not only earn more, but their wages and salaries have shown the best gains. By contrast, wages for many low-skilled workers have dropped (after adjusting for inflation).

• *The "real" incomes of most two-earner couples have consistently risen.* Among poorer workers, wives' earnings may offset some drop in their husbands' wages; but that isn't true at the top of the income spectrum or probably in the middle. In 1995, the median two-earner couple—the one in the middle of the income distribution—made $55,823, about 23 percent more in "real" dollars than a similar couple in 1970, says the Census Bureau. (Actual gains in purchasing power are even higher because the consumer price index, used to estimate real incomes, overstates inflation; therefore, it understates income.)

If men's wages suddenly surged, some wives might stampede back into the kitchen. Most would not. We've had an upheaval in attitudes and customs. Call it feminism, call it ambition, call it anything. Most women—and most men, too—now think that women should have the chance to work and pursue a career. In 1945, that wasn't true. As a society, we've created more social choices. In general, this is progress. It gives people more freedom to live as they see fit. But the new choices have spawned new anxieties, complaints, and complications.

One surprise is more economic inequality: a point made by Diana

Furchtgott-Roth of the American Enterprise Institute as well as Burtless. Well-paid workers increasingly marry each other and dominate the top of the income spectrum, while poorly paid workers increasingly don't marry (or don't have two workers) and drift toward the bottom. Between 1970 and 1995, the share of families with only a single mother rose from 11 to 18 percent. Since the late 1970s, these changes may explain about half of the increase in family income inequality, estimate Burtless and economist Lynn Karoly of the Rand Corp.

Another unintended consequence is that families do increasingly need two earners for a middle-class lifestyle, while only one was required for the 1950s' or 1960s' version. But here's the catch: Today's middle-class lifestyle is a lot richer. If people want to duplicate their parents' lifestyles, they can unplug their air conditioners, sell one of their cars, discard their VCRs and PCs, and stop sending all their kids to college. As more wives work, the two-earner couple becomes the norm. Couples still can have one partner stay at home, but only if they don't mind sliding down the income ladder or are exceptionally rich.

Let me give a simple example to show why. Suppose we have two sets of identical twins: Pete and Joe; and Mary and Sally. They marry. Pete weds Mary, and Sally takes Joe. They all have jobs, and each earns $35,000 a year. Each also gets a 10 percent increase every year. (I'm simply assuming away falling wages or inequality.) After five years, everyone earns almost $56,400; each couple's income is nearly $113,000. They buy identical houses and cars; they vacation together. They have the same lifestyles. Now Mary and Sally have babies—and Sally quits her job, while Mary (after maternity leave) goes back to work.

Watch what happens. Sally and Joe's income falls to 50 percent of Pete and Mary's. It doesn't make any difference that Joe still makes a good salary and that it's increasing 10 percent a year. Suddenly their lifestyles are no longer the same. Sally and Joe have trouble paying bills. Maybe they move to a smaller home; maybe they can't afford a new car or a vacation. Meanwhile, Pete and Mary, though comfortable financially, feel guilty about not spending more time with their baby. There's more tension as they try to juggle their schedules. And everyone wonders how Mom and Dad could have done it all while Mom stayed at home.

One reason is that Mom and Dad didn't live so well, materially. Another reason is that Mom didn't have much choice—and may occasionally have yearned to do something aside from making the bed, checking the homework, and cooking dinner. The larger point is that the dilemmas of the two-earner couple don't arise mainly because incomes (men's or otherwise) are growing slowly. People compare themselves to people like themselves. As more women work, the comparisons adjust quietly. It's women's wages, more than men's, that create pressures for women to work. We have more choices now than ever, but they aren't necessarily easier.

The Washington Post
January 22, 1997

THE DESERVING RICH?

Americans tend to view the rich the same way they view the poor. We split them informally into the deserving and the undeserving. We accept the deserving poor, because we deem them to be poor through no fault of their own. Similarly, the deserving rich enjoy our moral approval because they have somehow earned their wealth by enhancing society's well-being. On the other hand, the undeserving poor don't get much sympathy, because they're seen as responsible for their poverty, through laziness or dishonesty. Likewise, we dismiss the undeserving rich as having tumbled into their money accidentally, connived to get it, or misused it.

This distinction is a useful way to make sense of Americans' continuing obsession with the rich. Of this fascination, there can be no doubt. Forbes regularly catalogs the wealthiest 400 Americans. A recent book on the rich—*The Millionaire Next Door*—has been on *The New York Times* bestseller list for more than half a year and has 400,000 copies in print. And *Newsweek* recently ran a cover story on the "new rich," featuring the likes of Nike's Philip Knight (estimated worth: almost $6 billion) and Dell Computer's Michael Dell ($4 billion).

Americans generally don't despise the rich, according to polls assembled by Karlyn Bowman of the American Enterprise Institute. In one survey, 62 percent of respondents said the country benefits "from a class of rich people." Nor do most Americans think the rich have gotten that way by bleeding the poor or middle class. In another poll, only 30 percent thought that the rich "keep the common man from having his proper share of wealth." But on narrower issues, resentment emerges. About 80 to 90 percent of the public think professional athletes, movie stars, lawyers, and top executives are overpaid.

These attitudes seem unchanged from a century ago. In 1889, the British statesman James Bryce wrote in his classic *The American Commonwealth:* "There is in the United States no such general opposition as in Europe of . . . richer and poorer classes." He found little class "jealousy" or "hostility." Yet Bryce wrote in the midst of the populist movement that vilified business trusts and some of its tycoons, such as oil baron John D. Rockefeller.

The contradictions are less glaring than they seem. Getting rich is the end point of economic opportunity, and faith in the self-made person is a central part of the national folklore. Americans believe in ambition and don't reject those who fulfill their ambitions. If the victors in the economic struggle were all suspect, then the ideals of hard work, risk taking, and self-improvement would be illegitimate.

But we draw the line when wealth seems unrelated to effort, risk, or talent. For this reason, inherited wealth doesn't always command respect. Those who have it didn't earn it. They can establish their own worthiness by building constructively on the legacy of family money. Executive pay is often suspect because lavish bonuses and stock options may reflect corporate back-scratching: company directors pampering the CEO. When failed executives receive huge payoffs, ordinary Americans are gaga. The latest example is John Walter, who left as AT&T's president after nine months with a severance package valued at $26 million.

Similar doubts attach to the pay of athletes and movie stars. When Sandra Bullock earns (according to *People* magazine) $12.5 million for making *Speed II,* the rewards seem to exceed the talent. The same is true when the top professional quarterbacks make (according to the *Post*) $6.5 million a year, much more than some of the past greats (Johnny Unitas, Y. A. Tittle) got in their prime. So public skepticism is warranted. What makes today's athletes and stars more bankable is not larger talent or harder work, but TV and world-wide marketing.

We also object when wealth confers too much power. Americans have always distrusted concentrated power, in whatever form. John D. Rockefeller was disliked not because he was rich, but because, in getting rich, he destroyed many independent oil refiners and strove for monopoly. Bill Gates (estimated wealth, according to *Newsweek:* $36 billion) seems no different. Hardly anyone deplores the fact of his wealth. What unsettles people is that Microsoft may snuff out software rivals and control cyberspace.

Even the deserving rich may offend by flaunting their wealth. This violates another American ideal: Money doesn't measure human worth. Or as Jay Leno has said: Being wealthy means "you're just richer than everyone. It doesn't mean you're better." Not surprisingly, the superrich often strive to seem ordinary. Gates still comes across as the rumpled workaholic. In *The Millionaire Next Door,* authors Thomas Stanley and William Danko report that many of the wealthy "live below their means." By their estimate, about 3.5 percent of households have a net worth of $1 million or more.

"The large majority of these millionaires are not the descendants of the Rockefellers or the Vanderbilts," write Stanley and Danko. "More than 80 percent are ordinary people who have accumulated their wealth in one generation." These people are fairly frugal and value economic independence more than conspicuous consumption. Half have never spent more than $29,000 on a new car.

This is not, of course, the whole story. Getting money and making a point of what you've got is one way Americans keep score. Stanley and Danko argue many of the not-so-rich live above their means—buying expensive cars and flashy clothes—to project success. Scorekeeping is one cause of prominent feuds over huge sums: for example, the quest of *Seinfeld*'s supporting cast members for $1 million each per episode. It's not just that people want more; they also want to make a statement that they're better than the next star, the next quarterback, or the next CEO.

The wealthy often strive for more wealth than they can ever spend because they enjoy their work—and want to run up the score. That these contests can slip into greed or wretched excess should not surprise. The down-to-earth Gates is building a not-so-down-to-earth personal palace reckoned to be 35,000 square feet and to cost about $40 million. The contrasts will endure, because the rich, like the poor, will always be with us.

The Washington Post
August 13, 1997

PART VI

EXPERTS

THE TRIUMPH OF THE PSYCHO-FACT

We live in a world of real dangers and imagined fears. The dangers are often low and falling, while the fears are high and rising. We are hounded by what I call "psycho-facts": beliefs that, though not supported by hard evidence, are taken as real because their constant repetition changes the way we experience life. We feel assaulted by rising crime, increasing health hazards, falling living standards, and a worsening environment. These are all psycho-facts. The underlying conditions aren't true, but we feel they are, and therefore, they become so.

Journalists—trafficking in the sensational and the simplistic—are heavily implicated in the explosion of psycho-facts. But so are politicians, policy advocates, and promoters of various causes and lifestyles. Rarely do any of us deliberately lie. However, we do peddle incomplete or selective information that inspires misleading exaggerations or unwarranted inferences. People begin to feel that something's wrong, and this new sensation becomes an irrefutable fact or (worse) the basis for a misguided policy.

Crime? Yes, there's long been too much of it. But the best surveys do not show that it's dramatically worsened. Indeed, some victimization rates have dropped. The household burglary rate declined by 42 percent between 1973 and 1991. The number of annual murders has fluctuated between 20,000 and 26,000 since 1980; the major increase occurred in the 1960s, when the number doubled. A Gallup poll reports that 86 percent of the respondents haven't been victims of violent crime. By contrast, our consciousness of crime—fanned by local TV news—has risen.

On a recent network special, ABC correspondent John Stossel suggests we are "scaring ourselves to death." Psycho-facts are seductive precisely because they are often plausible. We've been told for years, for example, that our living standards are dropping, and this became a big Clinton theme in 1992. It isn't really so. Over any extended period, our living standards have risen. In the past 25 years, median family income is up by about one-fifth. But the rise is much slower than we expected—so slow that it's often imperceptible or nonexistent in any one year. We don't feel it.

Health, safety, and environmental hazards inspire similar misconceptions. Suppose an experiment shows that substance X causes cancer—at some dosage in some animal. We're soon worried that everything we eat or breathe containing the slightest trace of X is giving us cancer or heart disease. We feel that identifiable risks should be avoidable risks. We act as if there's a constitutional right to immortality and that anything that raises risk should be outlawed. Our goal is a risk-free society, and this fosters many outsized fears.

Lots of theoretical dangers (like asbestos or plane crashes) aren't large practical dangers. The easiest way to grasp this is to glance at the adjoining table. It compares relative risks of dying. What's worth remembering is that roughly 2.2 million Americans die every year. With about 260 million Americans, this means that in a crude arithmetic sense the average risk of dying is about one in 118 (2.2 million goes into 260 million 118 times). Now obviously, the old die in much greater numbers than the young. Still, the general risk of dying from natural causes or unavoidable accidents is much greater than the specific danger of many hazardous substances or jobs. (The table shows both.)

The Odds of Dying

Every year, about 1 in 100 of us dies. The dangers from high-profile risks like asbestos and plane crashes are relatively small.

For everyone	1 in 118
For those 35 to 44 years old	1 in 437
For police on the job	1 in 4,500
For women giving birth	1 in 9,100
From airplane crashes	1 in 167,000
From lightning	1 in 2 million
From asbestos in schools	1 in 11 million

Source: Robert Mitchell, Clark University. All data is annual.

Alarmists will point out that all the specific risks of dying create the overall risk of dying. True. But no matter how much we reduce any specific risk, we'll still die from something, and many specific risks aren't very threatening. In the ABC program, Stossel tweaks Ralph Nader for seeing danger almost everywhere: hot dogs have too much fat; airplanes aren't adequately maintained; coffee has caffeine; rugs collect dust and cause indoor pollution. "Life is preparedness—the old Boy Scout motto 'Be prepared,' " Nader says. The trouble is that if you spend all your life preparing, you may miss out on living.

Of course, we should take sensible personal precautions and enact prudent safety and environmental regulations. But they should be sensible and prudent. We should not overreact to every ghoulish incident or conceivable danger. The abduction and murder of Polly Klaas late last year was horrifying, but so was the kidnapping of the Lindbergh child in 1932. Cloistering children in generally safe neighborhoods is not a sensible reaction. The old, too, often sense-lessly barricade themselves indoors against imagined crime. We "give up some freedom," as Stossel says.

Likewise, misguided regulations based on exaggerated risk can waste lots of money. The asbestos panic was a costly mistake, as federal judge Stephen Breyer shows in a new book.* Leaving asbestos in buildings poses almost no hazard; removing it increases the danger by putting asbestos particles into the air. Breyer cites a toxic waste case where the company objected to the final cleanup. The site was already so clean that children could eat some dirt 70 days a year without significant harm. Why do more? "There were no dirt-eating children playing in the area," he writes, "for it was a swamp."

The standard retort is: A rich country like ours can afford absolute safety. No, we can't. Regulatory costs raise prices or taxes. Our incomes are lower than they might be. That's okay if we receive lots of benefits—much cleaner air or healthier food. But it's not okay if the benefits are trivial or nonexistent.

Good judgment requires good information. Every imagined danger or adverse social trend is not as ghastly as it seems. Consciousness-raising can be truth-lowering. We fall prey to our fears and fantasies. We create synthetic truths from a blend of genuine evidence, popular prejudice, and mass anxiety. Psycho-facts are not real facts. We should try to tell the difference.

Newsweek
May 9, 1994

* *Breaking the Vicious Circle: Toward Effective Risk Regulation* (Harvard University Press, 1995).

A NATION OF EXPERTS

There are many things in short supply in America, but experts are not among them. We are awash in experts: experts on politics, management, divorce, personal finance, terrorism, software, and much more. There are more experts today than yesterday, and there will be more tomorrow than today. If you are not yet a certified expert in something, you probably soon will be, and if you aren't, then you will qualify as a protected minority or endangered species. In America, not everyone can grow up to be president; but almost everyone can grow up to be an expert.

I had long suspected that this was true, but not until I stumbled across *The 1995 Yearbook of Experts, Authorities & Spokespersons* did I realize how true. The *Yearbook* amasses more than 900 pages of experts on everything from "Addictions/Boredom" (the Boring Institute) to "Bird Baths" (the National Bird Feeding Society) to "Health Fraud/Quackery" (the American Preventive Medical Association) to "Legal Issues/Hypnosis" (the American Council of Hypnotist Examiners) to "Relationships/Couples" (the Institute for Creative Solutions).

And the *Yearbook,* of course, just scratches the surface. James A. Smith, author of *The Idea Brokers: Think Tanks and the Rise of the New Policy Elite,* estimates that there are now about 1,200 public policy institutes. Many of them, plus a lot of universities and trade associations, publish their own guidebooks. Johns Hopkins University has a 301-page catalog of its experts, the Heritage Foundation's encyclopedia runs to 412 pages, and the American Council on Education has a pamphlet of 86 pages. As in most things, America leads the world in experts.

Just why this is so is a worthy subject of speculation. On one hand, the supply of potential experts has risen steadily. Americans have record numbers of degrees. In 1940, all colleges and universities awarded only 217,000 degrees, and most of those (187,000) were bachelors' degrees; there were only 27,000 masters' and 8,000 doctorates. By 1991, the total had passed 2 million, with 337,000 master's and 39,000 doctorates, including 430 Ph.D.s in "public affairs." Never before have so many Americans had a higher opinion of their own opinion than today.

Meanwhile, the demand for experts has exploded. We can mainly thank technology for this. Time was, for instance, when a lawyer might look forward only to a life of litigation or contract writing. No more. As the O. J. Simpson trial shows, a lawyer with a pretty face and a quick tongue can now anticipate becoming the legal equivalent of the late Howard Cosell. Ultimately, TV may peer into celebrated divorce cases or courtroom combat between corporations, so that these larger opportunities for lawyers will extend beyond ex-prosecutors or defense attorneys.

The O.J. trial symbolizes how technology has elevated our appetite for expertise. No one knows the exact number of talk radio shows, but Carol Nashe, executive vice president of the National Association of Radio Talk Show Hosts (listed on page 529 of the *Yearbook*), says there might be 5,000, national and local. Most need "guests," AKA "experts." Ditto for TV network news programs, talk shows, and newsmagazines. Someone has to fill the airtime on

Nightline. Cable TV, from the heights of *Larry King Live* on down, has further stimulated demand. Now, the Internet is doing the same.

And here's the real secret of America's success in cultivating experts: We trust the free market. Almost anyone can become an expert because no one says what an expert is or must know. If you can convince people of your bona fides—whatever they are—you triumph. Sure, credentials may help. Having a Ph.D. in astronomy might increase your odds of being called by *Nightline* if a new planet is discovered. But who knows? Maybe all you need is a backyard telescope. Anyway, you're free to bluff and bluster as far as you can.

The first step is to get listed in the *Yearbook of Experts.* There's a price, but it's modest. To be precise, it's $375. That buys a "reference listing," which is about a sixth of a page. If you want a bigger plug, a full page costs between $1,150 and $1,250. The whole process has been commercialized: you insert yourself in the book, which is sent free to a list of 14,000, including 1,400 daily newspapers and 1,200 news radio stations, TV stations, and magazines. Mitchell Davis, the *Yearbook's* editor and owner, likens it to "four mailbags of press releases."

He has, in effect, legitimized the do-it-yourself expert. Browsing through the *Yearbook,* you'll find the usual suspects, from Albert Shanker (head of the American Federation of Teachers) to the Edison Electric Institute (the trade group for utilities). But you'll also find Richard Carleton Hacker ("the Cigar Czar . . . the world's most entertaining author/spokesman on cigar smoking"), the National Anxiety Center (run by Alan Caruba, who monitors "media-driven 'scare campaigns' "), and Gary Martin ("forensic expert in boating and maritime accidents").

The expert explosion has led to some grousing that the process has gone berserk: that old authorities—calm, well informed, reasoned—are being displaced by loudmouths, self-promoters, and con artists. In an essay, Louis Menand, who teaches English at the City University of New York, complained that there has been a debasing of genuine expertise, because it is "almost automatically equated with elitism, and 'elite' has become the new scare word in American life." This is partly true, and our random process for anointing authorities has surely showered us with a lot of inept analysis, lousy advice, and pseudoscience.

But the larger truth is that new technology has disrupted the traditional enclaves of expertise, upsetting those who find its demands too time-consuming or demeaning. What matters now is not only what you know, but who hears you. Those who resist the constant calls for public blather find their status altered and often diminished. Alan Dershowitz may not be America's greatest legal authority, but he is among the best known because he is always camera-ready. In our status-conscious society, standing out from the crowd is an unrelenting ambition. Aspiring to expertdom is merely its latest expression.

Newsweek
June 5, 1995

THE WAY WE DIAPER

Johnny wears disposable diapers, and that's not an environmental disaster. By Johnny, I mean John Samuelson, who joined his sister, Ruth (five), and brother, Michael (three), eight weeks ago. I also mean most of the other nine million American babies under 30 months who wear disposable diapers. I do not feel guilty that my wife and I use them, and the idea that we are destroying the planet for our children is mostly nonsense.

Disposable diapers are an instructive metaphor for the exaggerations of modern environmentalism. We all should want to be good environmentalists, but just what that means in practice isn't always easy to say. The tendency these days is to call many different problems "environmental," as if the label—all by itself—implies an impending catastrophe whose solution is a moral imperative. "Environmentalism" thus becomes a loose collection of diverse concerns, with few distinctions made about whether some problems are more serious than others.

To call disposable diapers an environmental problem is to slide into this ambiguous and random alarmism. Disposable diapers are about garbage; that's ordinary garbage, not hazardous waste. Getting rid of our garbage is a problem and in some places a serious one. Mainly, it involves handling the trash at an acceptable cost. But this is not a crisis that threatens the earth's future, and even if it were, disposable diapers wouldn't matter much. The 15.8 billion used annually constitute less than 2 percent of all garbage.

These complexities are being lost in rising rhetoric. Disposable diapers have come to symbolize growing wastefulness, because most people still remember the era of reusable cloth diapers. Although Procter & Gamble first test-marketed Pampers in 1961, the product didn't go national until 1970. (P&G says that disposables now account for 90 percent of diapers, up from 65 percent in 1980 and 25 percent in 1970.) Vermont governor Madeleine Kunin has proposed banning disposables, though her legislature probably won't go along. And *Forbes* magazine recently lambasted them on its cover: "Can We Have a Cleaner Environment and Pampers Too?"

In fact, the symbolism is misleading. Our garbage problem is not primarily the result of our becoming an increasingly throwaway society. The Environmental Protection Agency estimates that the average American generates (after recycling) 3.3 pounds of garbage a day, only slightly higher than in 1970. The truth is that almost everything you probably believe about garbage is wrong, as archaeologist William Rathje, head of the Garbage Project at the University of Arizona, argues in December's *The Atlantic*.

You think plastics are the problem? Guess again. They account for about 8 percent of the garbage. Metals? They're about 9 percent. By contrast, paper represents 37 percent and yard waste 20 percent of garbage. Nor is today's problem especially bad historically. "Our society is filled with . . . reminders of waste," Rathje writes. "What we forget is everything that is no longer there to see . . . the 1,200 pounds per year of coal ash that every American generated at home at the turn of the century . . . [and] the hundreds of thousands of dead horses that once had to be disposed of by American cities every year."

The problem today stems from shifting societal standards. Landfills now absorb more than three-quarters of all garbage, and in a country as vast as ours, there's plenty of room for new ones. The trouble is that fewer communities want them, and tighter regulations are raising their costs. Between 1985 and 1988, average tipping fees—the cost of dumping a ton of garbage in a landfill—jumped from $12 to $27, reports the National Solid Wastes Management Association. Our task is to make landfills acceptable or find alternatives, from garbage prevention to recycling to incineration.

I have no quarrel with parents who prefer cloth diapers, as a rising minority apparently do. The National Association of Diaper Services reports its members' business is up about 40 percent in the past year. "I've never seen such a dramatic turnaround," says Jack Mogavero, president of General Health Care Corporation, the largest diaper service. (Environmentalism isn't the only reason. New diaper covers with Velcro closures make cloth diapers easier to use.) But parents are deluding themselves if they think that using cloth diapers is somehow saving the environment.

Suppose everyone switched to cloth diapers tomorrow. All those diapers (43 million a day, at current rates) have to be washed in hot water, which requires energy and generates pollution. For families using diaper services, the diapers have to be picked up and delivered by trucks that burn fuel, create fumes, and worsen traffic congestion. By contrast, most disposables are purchased in shopping trips that would be made anyway. The extra effects of higher energy consumption would be modest, but so is the impact of disposables on garbage.

The point is not to show that one diaper is environmentally superior to the other. It is simply to emphasize that comparisons are iffy. Each diaper does some damage, but how are we to judge relative dangers? Are air pollution and the threat to global warming more serious problems than garbage disposal? Environmental debates tend to slide by these messy choices.

My own hunch is that garbage is a lesser ill. To some extent, the problem—higher costs—is also the solution. As disposal costs rise, recycling becomes more attractive and economically viable. Carefully crafted, recycling laws aid the process by lowering collection costs. In 1988, about 31 percent of all paper was collected and reused. By 1995, the paper industry estimates, that could rise to 40 percent. There will be more efforts to cope with yard waste through mass composting rather than using landfills.

Personally, I'm doing my part within the bounds of common sense. Just last week I brought a coffee mug into the office. This will cut my use of polystyrene cups by somewhere between 300 to 600 a year. I want the best possible world for my new son, who has a beguiling smile and a calming stare. Relax, Dad, he says. Being a worrier, I can't. I already have lots of concerns for his future. But the way we diaper is not among them.

Newsweek
March 19, 1990

THE DADDY TRACK

Just the other night, my two-year-old son recorded his displeasure at my efforts to get him to bed. *"You keep quiet"*—he likes to shout—*"I throw you in the trash can."* So ends another day on the daddy track. It's about love, worrying, getting the kids dressed, and making them put away the toys. It's closely related to the mommy track.

This whole mommy track debate is a bit cockeyed. It quickly slides over or evades altogether the central issue, which is children. Having children is not an experience you can imagine in advance. Everyone else's children are not your children, and there's only one way to tell the difference. Parenting promotes perspective: it changes your view of life and (for some of us) what you want from it.

As most people understand it, the mommy track implies that mothers are sacrificing their careers—being shifted into less important jobs—because they're raising children. There are three things wrong with this notion. The first is that it involves "sacrifice." The second is that only mothers are affected. And the third is that decisions made in the early years of parenthood permanently doom careers.

My wife fits the stereotype of someone on the mommy track. Since our daughter's birth four years ago, she's been in and out of part-time jobs. She now has a job three days a week. But she doesn't think she's made a "sacrifice." My wife got off whatever "track" she was on because she wanted to. When my daughter arrived, I didn't suddenly lose all ambition. But I started getting home earlier at night, working less on weekends, and deferring (forever?) some bigger and enticing writing projects.

Both of us hope that what we're doing will help our children become more self-reliant and contented adults. Being a bit goofy, I'd like to think that we're even helping the country in a small way by raising responsible and productive citizens. Will any of this come true? Who knows? What is true is this: We're doing what we're doing because we also think it's good for us.

Just how modern fatherhood has changed (if at all) is something historians will ultimately decide. But there are signs that the once rigid parenting roles of provider and nurturer are blurring slightly. In a survey of its employees, Du Pont found that a rising number of young fathers were interested in issues such as child care. Many said they would avoid jobs involving frequent travel or relocation. Men are also doing more work at home. In the mid-1960s, women spent about four times as much time as men on housekeeping. By the early 1980s, the ratio was about two to one. Because men tend to have longer hours at full-time jobs than women, total work time is about equal.

Before I'm labeled a complete hypocrite, let me acknowledge the obvious: My wife has had to change more than I have. Despite my many admirable exertions (making the bed, doing the dishes, helping with the children at night), she still has most of the responsibility for the children. When not being thoroughly self-centered, I worry that she'll feel frustrated by the strains between home and job. But she doesn't worry—and neither do I—that once she returns to a full-time paid job, she'll have trouble finding something rewarding and challenging. Maybe she's lucky because she's in an expanding field, health care. But there's more to it, I think, than that.

Children grow up. Careers resume. This was hard when Betty Friedan's *The Feminine Mystique* appeared in 1963. It's vastly easier today—and will become more so tomorrow. "Women in the corporation are about to move from a buyer's to a seller's market," writes Felice Schwartz in the January–February *Harvard Business Review.* The baby boom has crested over the job market. Between now and 2000, labor force growth will be about two-thirds the rate of the early 1980s and less than half the rate of the 1970s. People with skills will be in high demand.

Here's something else: Today's young parents will probably have to work longer than their parents. The age at which retirees become eligible for full Social Security benefits is already scheduled to increase gradually from 65 to 67 between 2003 and 2027. As the population ages, the pressures to raise the retirement threshold further may grow. The period for child rearing will shrink in proportion to potential time in the job market.

It was Schwartz's article that triggered this debate. Without using the term *mommy track,* she seemed to support it by suggesting companies separate women into "career-primary" women (dedicated to their jobs) and "career-and-family" women (also eager to raise children). The separation would apparently be made before the children arrive. This is nutty. People can't know at 26 what they'll want or be like at 36 or 46. Otherwise, Schwartz's article is a sensible appeal that companies—to keep skilled workers—adopt policies to accommodate motherhood.

This is already happening, formally and informally. IBM recently said it would allow up to three years of personal leave for women and men. In a 1987 survey by the Labor Department, about half of all workplaces reported they had some policies intended to help parents (flexible working hours, part-time work, or job sharing). Could things be improved? Definitely. But personnel policies, no matter how enlightened, can never fully erase the conflicts between individuals and organizations.

Nor can they be legislated away, and the effort to do so is misguided. Government subsidies for child care would unfairly discriminate against families with mothers at home—roughly one out of two with children under age three. The view that such policies promote women's equality is misinformed. Sweden has the world's most extensive child care support programs. But Sweden's labor market "is sex segregated to an exceptional degree," reports a study from the Women's Research & Education Institute. Women are "rarely found in . . . management positions." Mothers still are mainly responsible for children.

Of course, children are the real reason these problems endure. Most children survive their parents' failings. But what about parents? You can't be at the sales meeting and Little League, to use Ellen Goodman's phrase. My children are exasperating, exhausting, and exhilarating. They are the best part of me, and I won't miss their growing up.

Newsweek
April 3, 1989

THE WAY THE WORLD WORKS

We are bombarded every New Year with dozens of prophecies. Some will come true, some will not. But what will almost certainly come true is that the most important trends and events of the next year won't have been predicted at all. This was so last year, when Asia's economic turmoil surprised almost everyone, and it's routinely so. Hardly anyone foresaw the collapse of communism, the advent of AIDS, the explosion of the Internet, and the sharp drops in crime and inflation. Our best seers are regularly humbled. Why is this?

One explanation, of course, lies in technical complexity. Who but an alert doctor would have known of the early AIDS cases and imagined how they might spread to millions? However, the same argument—understandable ignorance—cannot be made so easily of the Internet. A decade ago, millions of Americans used computers, but few foresaw the Internet's emergence. Even some presumed authorities (say, Bill Gates) initially misjudged its impact. This lapse highlights a larger source of our blunders: the way most of us view change.

We see it as boiling water. It proceeds slowly and predictably. The water warms, and it boils. But much change is abrupt and dramatic. It differs from what came before. Consider a few other scientific analogies. Pure water can be gradually lowered below its freezing point and remain a liquid. But touch it with anything, and it instantly turns to ice. It's a liquid one second, a solid the next. Or consider two chunks of uranium. Together, they're harmless. But rearrange the uranium atoms, and you can create a critical mass—and, conceivably, an atomic bomb. Life and history aren't always water coming slowly to a boil. Sometimes they're a critical mass triggering radical change.

We know now that Asia's booming economies had reached a critical mass leading to today's bust. Countries had made many poor investments—office towers in Thailand, factories in South Korea—that couldn't repay the funds used to build them. But in the reigning optimism of the "Asian miracle," no one connected the dots. A few bad projects were dismissed as isolated mistakes.

The chain reaction happened because something altered perceptions. Thailand devalued its currency in early July, admitting (in effect) that its problems were so widespread, it could no longer repay all its debts. Parallels were soon discovered in other countries. Fearing devaluations, domestic and foreign investors rushed to sell local currencies and stocks. The ensuing panic selling—which forced many currencies and stock markets down—made matters worse. But they were not (as many supposed) instances of runaway irrationality.

The Soviet collapse proceeded similarly. A repressive regime represses best when its cruelty is credible. Few challenge its authority. Rare dissenters are isolated, jailed, or killed with ease. They stand out. Hardly anyone hides or defends them. Everyone fears; many inform. The old Soviet Union earned its reputation for cruelty over many years: in the "liquidation" of kulaks (private farmers) in the late 1920s; in the millions of political prisoners sent to the gulags in the 1930s; in quelling uprisings in Hungary (1956) and Czechoslovakia (1968). But by the 1980s, the Soviet Union lost its capacity for boundless repression.

Solidarity's protest in Poland was not brutally put down. Political liberalization at home was tolerated and, under Gorbachev, encouraged. Perhaps this was a miscalculation. Or perhaps it reflected self-doubt among communist elites. Brezhnev once reportedly joked with Willy Brandt: "Do you know what Marx would say if he were alive today? 'Workers of the world, forgive me.' " Whatever, the change fostered a critical mass of opposition in Eastern Europe and Russia. Dissidents were emboldened. They multiplied and felt strength in numbers. Political control became harder. The rest is history.

What these cases involved was not instant upheaval but slow changes whose ultimate consequences went unrecognized because they 1) contradicted conventional wisdom; and 2) couldn't occur until they passed some unknown threshold. The same process may apply to some U.S. social and economic problems: they may reach—as Malcolm Gladwell has argued in *The New Yorker*—a "tipping point" after which they rise or fall rapidly. This, he says, may be true of crime. A hypothetical example shows why.

Assume a town starts with 100 criminals: Ten are caught each year, and 12 people become criminals. At first, crime rises slowly. In year one, it will be 2 percent higher. But after five years, it will be up 10 percent, and at some point (the tipping point), it could soar. Police are overwhelmed. They have a harder time solving crimes; more people become criminals and commit more crimes. Now reverse the assumptions. The town adds 20 percent more police, who catch 12 criminals a year. Longer prison terms deter people from crime; there are only ten new criminals a year. Crime drops slowly, but at some point it may plunge. Police solve and stop more crime. Fewer people become criminals.

All this may make falling crime rates a bit less mystifying (in 1997, Los Angeles had fewer than 600 murders for the first time since 1977, and murders in New York, 756 as of late December, were a third of their 1992 level). It may also explain unexpectedly low inflation (1.8 percent in the past year). Once companies believe government will reduce inflation, they act in ways—cutting costs, improving efficiency—that reduce inflation. Raising prices would make them uncompetitive. Similarly, some recent favorable trends (falling abortions and teenage pregnancies) could ultimately prove surprisingly large. As people change, the force of their example may influence others.

The lesson is that small changes feed on themselves, cause people (and institutions) to behave differently, and then crystallize into huge shifts. As Gladwell notes, not all change is linear—in a straight line. The belief in linear change survives because it makes everything seem simple and controllable. If we want warmer water, we just turn up the heat. This is not, however, the way the world usually works.

Newsweek
January 12, 1998

THE WORTHLESS IVY LEAGUE?

We all know that going to college is essential for economic success. The more prestigious the college, the greater the success. It's better to attend Yale or Stanford than, say, Arizona State. People with the same raw abilities do better and earn more by graduating from an elite school. The bonus flows (it's said) from better connections, brighter peers, tougher courses, or superior professors. Among many parents, the terror that their children won't go to the right college has supported an explosion of guidebooks, counselors, and tutoring companies to help students in the admissions race.

The trouble is that what everyone knows isn't true. Going to Harvard or Duke won't automatically produce a better job and higher pay. Graduates of these schools generally do well. But they do well because they're talented. Had they chosen colleges with lesser name-plates, they would (on average) have done just as well. The conclusion is that the Ivy League—a metaphor for all elite schools—has little comparative advantage. They may expose students to brilliant scholars and stimulating peers. But the schools don't make the students' success. Students create their own success; this makes the schools look good.

Evidence of this comes in a new study by Alan Krueger, an economist at Princeton, and Stacy Berg Dale, a researcher at the Andrew W. Mellon Foundation. Until now, scholarly studies had found that elite colleges lifted their graduates' incomes beyond their natural abilities. The bonus was about 3 to 7 percent for every 100 points of difference in SAT scores between schools. Suppose you go to Princeton and I go to Podunk; Princeton's SAT scores average 100 points higher than Podunk's. After correcting for other influences (parents' income, race, gender, SAT scores, high school rank), studies found that you would still earn a bit more. If I make $50,000, then you might make $53,500 (that's 7 percent).

But Dale and Krueger suspected that even this premium—not huge—might be a statistical quirk. The problem, they write, is that students who attend more elite colleges may have greater earnings capacity regardless of where they attend school. Characteristics important for admission may also be rewarded in the labor market. What might these be? Discipline. Imagination. Ambition. Perseverance. Maturity. Some exceptional ability. Admissions officers may detect these characteristics from interviews or course difficulty (different from grade average). But earlier studies didn't capture these factors.

To do so, Dale and Krueger examined the 1976 freshmen of 34 colleges. They ranged from Yale, Bryn Mawr, and Swarthmore (highest in SAT scores) to Penn State and Denison University (lowest in scores). The SAT gap between top and bottom was about 200 points. Dale and Krueger knew which colleges had accepted and rejected these students as well as their future earnings. By 1995, male graduates with full-time jobs earned an average of $89,026; women earned $76,859.

Dale and Krueger then compared graduates who had been accepted and rejected by the same (or similar) colleges. The theory was that admissions officers were ranking personal qualities, from maturity to ambition. Students who fared similarly would possess similar strengths; then, Dale and Krueger compared the earnings of these students—regardless of where they went. There was no difference. Suppose that Princeton and Podunk accept you and me; but you go to Princeton and I go to Podunk. On average, we will still make the same. (The result held for blacks and whites, further weakening the case for race-based admission preferences. The only exception was poorer students, regardless of race; they gained slightly from an elite school.)

The explanation is probably simple. At most colleges, students can get a good education if they try. An able student who attends a lower-tier school can find able students to study with, write Dale and Krueger. Similarly, even elite schools have dim-wits and deadbeats. Once you're in the job market, where you went to college may matter for a few years, early in your career. Companies don't know much about young employment candidates. A shiny credential (an Ivy League degree) may impress. But after that, what people can or can't do counts for more. Skills grow. Reputations emerge. Companies prefer the competent from Podunk to the incompetent from Princeton.

If you can't (or won't) take advantage of what Princeton offers, Princeton does no good. What students bring to college matters more than what colleges bring to students. The lesson has relevance beyond elite schools. As a society, we've peddled college as a cure for many ills. Society needs more skilled workers. So, send more students to college. College graduates earn much more than high school graduates. So—to raise incomes—send more students to college. In that, we've succeeded. Perhaps three-quarters of high school graduates go to college, including community colleges.

But half or more don't finish. A new study from the Department of Education ("College for All?") reports that these students achieve only modest gains in skills and income. What determines who finishes? In another report, Clifford Adelman—a senior researcher at the Department of Education—finds that the most powerful factor is the difficulty of high school courses. And the finding is strongest for black and Hispanic students. Not having enough money (inadequate financial aid) explains few dropouts. Tough courses do more than transmit genuine skills. They provide the experience—and instill the confidence—of completing something difficult.

How to motivate students to do their best? How to make high schools demanding while still engaging? How to transmit important values (discipline, resourcefulness, responsibility) to teenagers, caught in life's most muddled moment? These are hard questions for parents and society as a whole. If the answers were self-evident, we'd have already seized them. But going to college—even Harvard—is no shortcut.

Newsweek
November 1, 1999

THE INTERNET AND GUTENBERG

In our self-absorbed age, everything is the newest New Thing or the biggest Big Thing. This spirit inevitably invests the Internet with transcendent significance. Steve Case of America Online already calls the new century "the Internet century," and some authorities whisper that the Internet rivals the importance of Gutenberg's invention of the printing press in the fifteenth century. We suffer from historical amnesia.

Suppose you were born in 1900. You wouldn't yet watch movies (the first big silent hit, *The Great Train Robbery,* showed in 1903), let alone imagine global TV. The airplane hadn't been invented, and Henry Ford wouldn't produce the first Model T until 1908. Less than 10 percent of U.S. homes had phones, and less than 8 percent had electricity. Antibiotics hadn't been discovered. As yet, the Internet isn't in the same league with these developments.

Each changed lifestyles and popular beliefs. The automobile suburbanized America and inaugurated mass travel. Antibiotics, vaccines, and public health advances helped raise life expectancy from 47 in 1900 to 77 today. The explosion of prosperity—a consequence of electricity, other technologies, and modern management—shortened working hours and expanded leisure. Movies and TV transformed popular culture.

The Internet is too young for anyone to foretell its ultimate significance, and time might vindicate the brashest prophecies. But some present claims aren't true. It is not true that no major innovation has spread so quickly. In 1990, only a handful of computer buffs used the Internet; by 1999, perhaps 38 percent of households were connected, reports Morgan Stanley Dean Witter. This roughly matches the adoption of the radio (which went from 0 to about 46 percent of households in the 1920s) and lags TV (which went from 9 percent of households in 1950 to 87 percent in 1960).

Of course, the Internet is a work in progress. If nothing else, the America Online–Time Warner merger is a gamble on the next generation of Internet technology. At present, most home users have dial-up service through modems and old phone lines. The replacement technology is "broadband," which—through enhanced cable lines, fiber optics, satellites, or better phone lines—would sharply raise transmission speeds. A fast phone modem today would allow a 10-megabyte file (equivalent to a 10- to 20-minute movie clip) to be downloaded in 24 minutes, says the Federal Communications Commission. Faster cable lines can do the same job in about a minute.

The Internet, television, and the telephone will blend. This, at any rate, is the conventional wisdom. For AOL–Time Warner, the grand strategy is to provide both transmission services (Time Warner owns the second largest cable system) and "content" (from Internet services to films, TV programs, magazines, music—or something entirely new). Other companies harbor similar ambitions. But we don't know whether this vision, or some other, will materialize.

Technologies acquire historical weight by reshaping the human condition. Gutenberg's press led to mass literacy, fostered the Protestant Reformation (by undermining the clergy's theological monopoly), and, through the easy exchange of information, enabled the scientific revolution. In the nineteenth century railroads created a truly national American market that favored mass production and the consumer society. To join this league, the Internet must be more than e-mail or a marketing platform. If you buy a book or car on the Net, the critical part of the transaction is still the book or car. Especially in business-to-business commerce, the Internet may improve efficiency through more price competition and supplier choice. But these are changes of degree, not kind.

Thoughtful Internet enthusiasts offer plausible speculations about its greater meaning. "Over the past 200 years, we have built up industrial economies of mass production . . . and mass markets," says Esther Dyson, editor of *Release 1.0,* a newsletter. By providing so much information, the Internet empowers consumers to escape mass markets; by making information so easy to dispense, it enables people to become independent producers. "The major impact is to give individuals more power over their lives," she says, while making it "tougher for governments, businesses—anyone—to operate in secrecy."

Kevin Kelly of *Wired* magazine, author of *New Rules for the New Economy,* argues that the "Internet is actually being underhyped. Of all the people online in ten years, only a tenth are online today." This could accelerate global commerce and weaken (for good or ill) national governments.

All the large issues remain unsettled. Will the Net enhance individual autonomy—or infringe on privacy? Will it increase people's economic independence—or expand corporate power (America Online–Time Warner would be no pygmy)? Before answers become clear, the Internet will have to attain economic viability. Though booming, it is now largely a capitalist charity. Almost everything on it is being given away or sold at a loss. Retail e-commerce is puny. In 1999, it amounted to less than .5 percent of U.S. consumer spending. Ditto for advertising. In 1999, Internet ads amounted to $1.8 billion out of total U.S. advertising of $215 billion, estimates Robert Coen of Universal McCann.

The great Internet fortunes arise mainly from stock speculation or building the infrastructure—supplying computers, software, and fiber optics. In 1999, this spending was $366 billion, says Nortel

Networks, a major supplier. Sooner or later, the investment must pay a return, or it will stop. Even if the Internet flourishes, it may remain smaller than earlier Big Things. Our historical amnesia could benefit from the words of a Tennessee farmer at a church meeting in the 1940s. "Brothers and sisters, I want to tell you this," he said. "The greatest thing on earth is to have the love of God in your heart, and the next greatest is to have electricity in your home." Can the Internet really top that?

Newsweek
January 24, 2000

DON'T HOLD YOUR BREATH

Global warming may or may not be the great environmental crisis of the next century, but—regardless of whether it is or isn't—we won't do much about it. We will (I am sure) argue ferociously over it and may even, as a nation, make some fairly solemn-sounding commitments to avoid it. But the more dramatic and meaningful these commitments seem, the less likely they are to be observed. Little will be done. I wouldn't stake my life on that, but I don't see how it could turn out otherwise.

Democracies can't easily make present sacrifices to avoid future menaces. We require (it seems) a clear and present danger, if not a crisis, to stir us to action. This is why we won't soon mobilize against global warming. The politics simply won't compute. To do something effective would require a heavy energy tax or its equivalent. A good round figure for a tax is $100 per ton of carbon; this would raise gasoline prices an estimated 26 cents a gallon and electricity and natural gas rates by almost 30 percent. The idea would be to dampen energy use and the emission of greenhouse gases (mostly carbon dioxide) from the burning of fossil fuels (oil, coal, gas).

To put it mildly, the odds of Congress's passing such a tax are low. The problem with global warming is that we don't know yet whether it represents a genuine national threat and, if so, how large. Congress might conceivably react to a legitimate threat, even if distant. But it won't impose pain on voters for no obvious gain to solve a hypothetical problem. And if the United States won't, neither will anyone else. We generate the most greenhouse gases, about 22 percent of the annual total. Other countries won't squeeze themselves to preserve our lifestyles.

I talked last week to global warming believers and skeptics. Despite policy differences, they tend to agree about the modest state of current knowledge. Here's what we know. Since the dawn of the Industrial Age (say, 1800), the concentration of carbon dioxide in the atmosphere has risen about 30 percent. In the past century, average surface temperatures have increased 1 degree Fahrenheit (.5 degree Celsius). The widespread suspicion is that these trends are connected. Industrial and transportation emissions increased carbon dioxide, trapping more heat in the atmosphere and raising temperatures. The rival theory is that the small temperature rise is a natural climatic variation.

Now, here's what we don't know:

• *We don't know how much—or if—temperatures might rise in the next century.* In 1995, the United Nations' Intergovernmental Panel on Climate Change predicted that average temperature might increase between 1 degree C and 3.5 degrees C, with the best guess at 2 degrees C. Even this huge variation is hedged with qualifications and isn't accepted by many scientists, because it's based on admittedly crude computer simulations of climate.

• *We don't know—despite much scare talk—what the effects of warming might be.* The computer models can't predict the exact impact on regions or precise shifts in storm patterns. Warmer weather might make some areas more attractive and others less. Hotter weather could depress crop output in some places and raise it in others.

• *We don't know how to prevent warming.* Once greenhouse gases reach the atmosphere, they tend to stay there. So stabilizing annual emissions isn't enough; they have to be cut sharply. But economic growth requires more energy, and fossil fuels provide 85 percent of all energy. Without a breakthrough in alternative energy—nuclear, solar, something—no one knows how to lower emissions adequately without ultimately crushing the world economy. (By 2050, emissions might have to drop 50 percent or more from expected levels.)

The idea that global warming is a certain calamity simply isn't proven. Anyone who thinks otherwise should read Richard A. Kerr's superb story in the May 16 issue of *Science* magazine ("Greenhouse Forecasting Still Cloudy"). In it, he illuminates the doubts that plague computer modeling of climate. By altering a few assumptions, one model cuts its forecast of global warming caused by a doubling of CO_2 concentrations from 5.2 degrees C to 1.9 degrees C. Based on present knowledge, the best way of coping with warming—if it happens—would be to adapt to it. Change would probably occur over decades. If sea levels rose because oceans warmed, coastal areas would erect retaining walls—or people would move. Farmers would adjust crops to new weather.

I write all this as someone who actually favors an energy tax, mainly for national security reasons (to cut dependence on insecure Mideast oil). I believe that, within limits, we could improve energy efficiency without wrenching changes in lifestyles or high economic costs. Well, we had two oil crises in the 1970s and fought a war in the 1990s over oil. None of these events spurred a major energy tax, and global warming would ultimately demand a bigger tax. (A $100-per-ton carbon tax, for example, might cut CO_2 emissions back only to 1990 levels by 2010.)

What I conclude is that global warming promises to become a gushing source of national hypocrisy. President Clinton recently fulminated to the United Nations about the dangers of global warming without specifying how the United States might combat it. Late this year, an international conference will try to fashion a global treaty. Already 65 senators have signed a resolution sponsored by West Virginia senator Robert Byrd rejecting any treaty that doesn't demand emission cuts by poor countries (China, India, etc.). But these countries have—temporarily—been exempted for good reasons. They didn't cause most greenhouse gases, and penalizing their development would perpetuate their poverty.

The difference between Clinton and Byrd is less than it seems. Clinton wants to seem engaged without doing much; Byrd et al. want to find a respectable reason (i.e., poor countries aren't participating) for being disengaged. Hardly anyone wants to admit candidly the uncertainties of global warming. It's politically incorrect to question whether this is a serious problem that serious people ought to take seriously. But it would be political suicide to do anything serious about it. So shrewd politicians are learning to dance around the dilemma.

Newsweek
July 14, 1997

THE JOBS ARE THERE

Sociologist William Julius Wilson's new book, *When Work Disappears: The World of the New Urban Poor,* will appeal to believers in huge government programs as antidotes to our worst social problems. Wilson contends that a lack of jobs explains the black "underclass." Work imposes "disciplines and regularities," he writes. The fact that 30 to 60 percent of men in the poorest ghettos may not have jobs drives crime and family breakdown. Wilson wants a new Works Progress Administration (the Depression's public works agency) to fill the job gap.

Wilson—who recently moved to Harvard from the University of Chicago—isn't naive. He knows that his proposal defies today's antigovernment climate. He rightly isn't cowed; academics shouldn't pander to political fads. The real problem is with his theory. It's wrong. The jobs are there. Since 1980, the U.S. economy has created more than 27 million of them. Most men, whatever their race, shouldn't regularly be without work. If they are, the main reason is that they lack the skills, discipline, or desire to find and keep jobs.

For blacks, there are other contributing causes: racial prejudice, poor schools, and the suburbanization of jobs. But the basic availability of work is confirmed by most Afro-Americans, who have jobs. The single-minded focus among scholars and reporters on the "underclass" has unwittingly fed the worst racial stereotypes. No one ever seems to succeed; everyone seems to be on the brink of joblessness and starvation. In fact, the record—though hardly perfect—is much better:

• *Among those 25 and older, employment rates for blacks and whites are similar.* In 1995, 64 percent of whites had jobs and 61 percent of blacks—with the gap larger for men than for women. Although unemployment for blacks older than 25 is about twice the white level (7.4 percent vs. 3.9 percent), rates converge as education levels rise. Among college graduates, it was 2.3 percent for whites and 3.2 percent for blacks. (Employment and unemployment rates don't total 100 percent, because many people—students, homemakers, retirees—aren't in the labor market.)

• *The largest racial differences in employment rates now occur among the young.* Of those age 16 to 24 not enrolled in school, about 75 percent of whites are working; the employment rate for blacks is only 56 percent. Fewer blacks look for work, and among those who do, the unemployment rate is more than twice as high.

• *Although blacks earn on average less than whites, the largest income gaps exist between blacks and blacks.* Among married couples with children where both husband and wife work, median wages for blacks in 1995 were $836 a week—86 percent of the level for white couples. But that was three times the median wage of working single-parent black mothers—$287. The trouble is that 44 percent of black families with children are headed by single women; for whites, the figure is 15 percent.

The economy can't explain all that's gone wrong. The decline in marriage extends beyond the "underclass." Crime afflicts many teenagers well before they might become workers. Shifts in popular culture seem to have hurt blacks the most: marriage's reduced importance, the declining stigma of out-of-wedlock births, the sense that society "owes" everyone a good job, the greater tolerance (as Senator Daniel Patrick Moynihan puts it) of greater deviance. These are the seeds of social decay.

If men aren't responsible for their children, they feel less pressure to work. If crime is high among young blacks, even noncriminals will have a harder time getting work. The image of the worst subtly attaches to the best. High inner-city joblessness is a consequence of these trends more than a cause. True, as Wilson argues, cities' loss of manufacturing has cost blacks jobs. But inner-city unemployment has risen even in cities (such as Washington) that never had many factories. One reason, as Wilson notes, is that successful blacks often leave. Consider three Chicago neighborhoods that he's studied. Between 1950 and 1990, their population dropped from 250,000 to 86,000.

Wilson is correct that, for those who are left, the economic prospects are worse. Informal job networks are weak. Reaching suburban employers takes longer. Social pressure to have a job is less. Job discrimination hurts. Young inner-city black men often are seen as lazy or dishonest.

Not all of this reflects racial prejudice, Wilson argues. He reports that in surveys of Chicago companies, black employers had the same negative views as whites. So did many inner-city residents. "About 65 percent of black males . . . don't wanna work hard—they want a real easy job, making big bucks," a 30-year-old employed father said.

Somehow, though, many blacks (and whites, too) who don't have work in their early 20s get it by their early 30s. It's also hard to argue, as Wilson once did, that the declining economic status of black men caused family breakdown by making men less attractive husbands. The flaw is that, over time, the economic status of black men has risen. Since World War II, hundreds of occupations (from accountants to reporters) that were once barred to blacks have been opened. In 1995, the median wage for black men was 73 percent of the median wage for whites. But this ratio was 43 percent in 1940 and 64 percent in 1970.

Wilson minimizes (by omission) this sort of incomplete progress, perpetuating the idea that jobs must be provided rather than pursued. His book can be read as part of a civil war raging in the black community, as it is in the larger society. The struggle pits those who care about middle-class values—work, family, responsibility—against those who don't. Wilson cares and hopes that more jobs will create better values. His theory aims to justify a radical jobs agenda to advance conservative goals.

It's also a desperate agenda that, though understandable, simply assumes away the most stubborn aspects of inner-city poverty. Some proposals seem disconnected from common sense. At one point, Wilson endorses a scheme to provide public jobs "for low-skilled jobless workers" as "day care aides and playground assistants." All races would qualify. But who'd want to entrust their children to the least responsible and capable workers, regardless of race? This is a triumph of hope over reason.

The Washington Post
September 11, 1996

PART VII

THE PRESS

DOWN WITH THE MEDIA ELITE!?

The future of people like me was better in the past—or so it seems. By "people like me," I mean the folks in the mass media: newspapers, magazines, and network TV. Even as we're courted and castigated for our alleged power, new communications and computer technologies threaten our incomes, social importance, and political influence. This will gratify those who see us as an unelected "media elite" that is poisoning politics and culture. The rival view is that the mass media help bind the country together with shared experiences and information. It may not matter which view is more correct; the new technologies aren't listening and don't care.

Until now, I doubted that the new media much menaced the old. Cable, computers, and fiber optics delivered specialized information—on everything from stocks to diseases—that wouldn't displace general news and entertainment. Perhaps. But two events have shaken my confidence. The first is a survey from the Pew Research Center for the People & the Press showing big changes in our media habits. Most startling is the eclipse of the TV networks' nightly news programs. In 1993, 60 percent of Americans over 18 "regularly" watched; by 1998, this was 38 percent. Some of the loss reflected less interest in news, but much of it stemmed from more viewing—during the day—of cable news. Similarly, Internet use has soared. In 1995, 4 percent of adults went on-line to get news once a week; now, that's 20 percent.

My second jarring event was a chat with my brother Richard. He runs a small inn in Cape May, New Jersey. In the past year, he started advertising on the Internet with his own Web site. He's never seen anything like it; almost a fifth of his customers found the inn on-line. No magazine or newspaper ad ever showed remotely similar results. And the Internet is inexpensive. He paid less than $1,000 to a small company in Indianapolis to create and maintain the site for a year. "On the Internet, you compete equally [with bigger inns and hotels]," he says. "You have a page, and they have a page."

Hmmm. The mass media exist for only two reasons. One is that people read us or watch us; the other is that people and companies use us to advertise. These are, of course, connected. If people don't read or watch us, advertisers won't use us. But if advertisers don't use us—for whatever reason—then we will lose our audiences. Advertising pays the bills. Newspapers, for example, receive 70 to 80 percent of their revenues from ads (circulation is most of the rest). If ads evaporate, the mass media won't be able to afford the programs and news staffs that attract audiences.

I had assumed that at least newspapers and magazines were safe, because paper is so superior to screens for reading and relaxing. You can take a newspaper or magazine with you. You can fold it or clip it. If you lose it, no big deal. How could a screen, no matter how portable, compete with that? It couldn't—as long as people read as I do. Reading is (for me) a discrete experience; I settle back with a paper or book. But suppose habits change? This happens. TV decimated evening newspapers. Between 1950 and 1997, their number went from 1,450 to 816; their circulation dropped two-thirds.

We may now be at a similar inflection point. The Pew survey doesn't tell us where we're going, but it suggests that we're moving from where we've been. People can get more information than ever in more ways than ever; so they may change what they get and how. Generations seem to regard "news" and "information" differently. Among those 18 to 29, three-quarters told Pew they like "having so many information sources," but only a third enjoy "keeping up with the news." Among those over 65, only half like more information sources, but two-thirds enjoy keeping up with the news.

So habits may change. Suppose people progressively take more and more news from their computers; they call up headlines, commentary, or movie reviews between e-mails at work or games at home. Will fewer people then want newspapers? Already readership has eroded. Between 1970 and 1997, the share of adults who read a daily paper slipped from 78 to 59 percent. Or suppose people can customize their papers electronically. You preselect what you want—say, six top national and global stories, four top local stories, two favorite columnists, seven stock prices, the baseball standings, and your horoscope. It's zapped to your home and printed on 8½-by-11 paper. Is this still a newspaper?

We don't know what new technologies will bring (or when), because they're constantly evolving. Nor do we know what people want. Being cyber doesn't guarantee success. In March the on-line magazine *Slate* began charging $19.95 a year for what it had been giving away; estimated readership fell from more than 200,000 to less than 30,000. In the present economic boom, both new and old survive. But in leaner times, competition will be less forgiving, and even now the shift from mass audiences is unmistakable.

Magazines' growth has come mainly from new titles—aimed at smaller audiences—and not more readers of mass magazines. *Newsweek*'s circulation in 1998 (3.2 million) is almost the same as in 1978 (3 million). At the TV networks, audiences are approaching free fall. Here is where economics and sociology intersect. The notion of a media elite, if ever valid, requires that people get news and entertainment from a few sources dominated by a handful of executives, editors, anchors, reporters, and columnists. As media multiply, the elite becomes less exclusive. Smaller audiences give them less prominence and market power (i.e., salaries).

There is a logic here that, for the moment, seems to be suspended or even defied. The star system thrives, especially in TV but also in print journalism. Katie Couric's new contract pays her a reported $7 million a year; *Variety* puts Jane Pauley's latest contract at about $5.5 million a year. These huge amounts measure the desperation of media companies, which will pay small fortunes to anyone or for anything (the NFL, *ER*) that, they hope, will arrest the loss of audience. This is a rear-guard action. Sooner or later, the logic may assert itself and we in the mass media may find our net worth and self-worth correspondingly reduced.

Newsweek
July 13, 1998

DO SMOKERS HAVE RIGHTS?

The media are deeply sensitive to the rights of "minorities": the poor, the disabled, blacks, gays, and immigrants, among others. But there is one minority much larger than any of these (at least 25 percent of the population) whose rights we deny, ignore, or minimize: smokers. The debate over cigarettes has been framed as if smokers are the unwitting victims of the tobacco industry. They lack free will; therefore their apparent desires, opinions, and interests don't count. They are to be pitied and saved. But they are not to be respected.

This is, once again, pack journalism run amok. We media types fancy ourselves independent and skeptical thinkers. Just the opposite is often true: we're patsies for the latest social crusade or intellectual fad. In this case, the major media have adopted, perhaps unconsciously, the view of the public health community, which sees smoking as a scourge to be eradicated. The "story" is the crusade; the villain is the tobacco industry. Coverage is selective. Lost are issues that ought to inform this debate.

The simplest is whether, in trying to make Americans better off, the antismoking crusade would make many Americans worse off.

Smokers would clearly suffer from huge price and tax increases. The cost of the $368.5-billion agreement between the tobacco industry and the state attorneys general is estimated at 62 cents a pack. President Clinton suggests raising that to $1.50 a pack—about six times today's tax (24 cents). The cost would fall most heavily on poorer people. They smoke more than the rich and spend more of their smaller incomes on cigarettes.

Consider. About half (53 percent) of today's cigarette tax is paid by taxpayers with incomes of less than $30,000, estimates the congressional Joint Committee on Taxation. Only 1 percent is paid by those with incomes over $100,000. Higher prices will deter some people from smoking. But for the rest, would siphoning billions away from poorer people be good policy? Or fair?

The antismoking crusaders try to seem fair by arguing three things: 1) there's growing smoking among teenagers, who, once they try cigarettes, may become addicted for life; 2) tobacco ads cause much teen smoking—teens are, therefore, victims; and 3) passive smoking (the inhaling of smoke by nonsmokers) in public places is a serious health threat, justifying action against smokers. These assumptions also permeate media coverage, but the first two are open to question and the third is untrue.

Start with teen smoking. One survey from the University of Michigan does show a rise. In 1996, 34 percent of 12th graders reported smoking in the past month: the highest since 1979 (34.4 percent) and higher than in the late 1980s (29.2 percent). But the government's survey on drug abuse reports the opposite: in 1996, only 18.3 percent of teens between 12 and 17 had smoked in the past month, the lowest since the question was first asked in 1985 (29 percent). It's hard to know which survey to believe. But neither depicts runaway teen smoking. Even by the Michigan survey, the smoking rate is below that of the late 1970s (37 percent).

As for ads, teens do a lot of dangerous things (drugs, early sex) that aren't advertised and are often illegal. The tobacco industry no doubt targets teens; but the ads may affect brand choices more than the decision to smoke. A new, comprehensive study of youth health—financed by the National Institutes of Health—suggests that other forces are more important in determining who smokes.

"Time and time again, the home environment emerges as central in shaping health outcomes for American youth," it says. "Children who report feeling connected to a parent are protected against many different kinds of health risks including: emotional distress and suicidal thoughts and attempts; cigarette, alcohol and marijuana use; violent behavior; and early sexual activity."

And even teens who smoke do not necessarily become lifetime smokers. Among 12th graders, about twice as many (63 percent) once smoked as currently smoke. Quit rates are higher for adults. The "addiction" isn't so great that millions haven't broken it.

Finally, passive smoking isn't a big public health risk, as many stories imply. The latest example of misreporting involved a study from the Harvard Medical School. It purported to show that passive smoking doubled the risk of heart attacks, indicating a huge public health problem. That's how both *The New York Times* and *The Washington Post* reported it. In fact, the study—at most—showed that passive smoking doubles a very tiny risk.

Here's why. The study followed 32,046 nonsmoking nurses between 1982 and 1992. Of these, four-fifths said they were exposed to passive smoking. But there were only 152 heart attacks (127 nonfatal) among all the nurses: a small number. Many heart attacks would have occurred even if no one had been exposed to smoke. Ichiro Kawachi, the lead investigator, estimates that passive smoking caused perhaps 25 to 30 percent of attacks: that's 38 to 46 cases. If true (and the study has potential flaws), the practical significance of this is negligible. Most exposure to passive smoke is now private or voluntary, because public smoking has been barred in so many places. Are we going to outlaw husbands smoking in front of their wives—or vice versa?

You don't hear much of any of this, because the press has generally parroted the self-serving assumptions of antismoking crusaders. They have a case. Smoking is highly risky for smokers; if no one smoked, more Americans would live longer. But lots of things are risky, and one central question is whether smokers have a right to engage in behavior whose pleasures and pains are mainly theirs without being punished by the rest of society. Or are they to be persecuted?

There is almost no one to make the smokers' case. They have been abandoned by the tobacco industry, which wants a settlement. Most politicians won't defend smokers for fear of being cast as stooges of a bad industry and enemies of good health. And the press has blessed the whole process in its latest spasm of group-think. It has popularized the fiction that this debate is mainly between the tobacco industry and public health. The murkier reality is that, for better or worse, smokers are the main targets. Do they have rights? Apparently not.

The Washington Post
September 24, 1997

ALL BECAUSE OF A DEFECTIVE LAW

As it happens, the story behind the story may ultimately be more important than the story itself. The "story" is President Clinton's impending grand jury testimony. The unseen story is how a dubious law—here, the law of sexual harassment—takes us in unintended and unwanted directions. Most Americans wish they'd never heard of Monica Lewinsky. A CBS news survey last week found that, by a 63 to 31 percent margin, people think the country would be better off if the Lewinsky investigation had never started. The reason it did is sexual harassment law.

The scandal began with the Paula Jones lawsuit—a case that never should have been brought. By saying that, I don't mean to condone what Clinton is alleged to have done and what, I suspect, he actually did. If he propositioned Jones, he behaved crudely. If he had an affair with Lewinsky, he acted recklessly. If he lied about it, he was foolish. Clinton's problems stem mostly from Clinton's character. Still, the scandal has illuminated the large defects of sexual harassment law.

To say that the Jones case never should have been brought does not mean that it was frivolous. A frivolous case involves behavior that didn't occur or, if it did, is legal. But the law on sexual harassment is so murky and expansive that it extends to Jones's complaint (that Clinton asked for oral sex). The law makes almost any kind of unwanted sexual speech or conduct potentially illegal if, somehow, it's tied to the workplace.

Ugly things do happen at work. A recent *Washington Post* poll found that 56 percent of Americans think women are "often" harassed at work. But good things happen, too. Although a lot of office romances end poorly, the most likely outcome is marriage, reports a survey of 600 corporate personnel officers by the Society for Human Resource Management. It would be nice to have a law that prevented—or punished—abusive sexual behavior at work without suppressing men's and women's freedom to deal naturally with each other. Present law doesn't approach this lofty ideal.

The central problem is that no one can say what sexual harassment is. Just about everyone agrees that supervisors shouldn't ask subordinates for sexual favors in return for a job, higher pay, or a promotion. This is "quid pro quo" harassment. But the law goes beyond this and makes feelings—anger, embarrassment, displeasure—the basis for claiming "hostile environment" harassment. The result is to convert boorish behavior, botched relationships, and bad taste into grounds for lawsuits. Just what's legal and illegal is completely muddled.

How muddled? Congress doesn't mention harassment in Title VII of the 1964 Civil Rights Act, which prohibits job discrimination. The Supreme Court more or less invented the concept but doesn't clearly say what it is. The court defines harassment as conduct "so severe or pervasive as to alter the conditions of [the victim's] employment and create an abusive work environment." When "properly applied," this standard would "filter out complaints attacking the ordinary tribulations of the workplace, such as the sporadic use of abusive language, gender-related jokes, and occasional teasing."

Got it? Well, let's apply it to Clinton's alleged behavior toward Jones. Although it wasn't "pervasive" (there was one incident), it seems "severe." Having your boss drop his pants and ask for oral sex goes beyond work's "ordinary tribulations." Yet U.S. District Judge Susan Webber Wright dismissed Jones's suit on the grounds that this incident, if true, does "not constitute the kind of sustained and non-trivial conduct necessary for a claim of hostile work environment." Got it? (Jones has appealed.)

I am in the uneasy position of agreeing with Wright's result while suspecting she willfully misread the law. If Clinton headed the local power company, would she have let him off? I doubt it. But the real point is that no one can tell; the standard is that vague. I think Jones's suit never should have been brought, because the law should be tighter. Harassment should involve job consequences—either the threat or loss of a job or pay. (Jones suffered none, despite claims to the contrary.) But that's not the law now, and as a result, it does more harm than good.

Eugene Volokh of the UCLA Law School offers much evidence that free speech is suppressed in the name of halting harassment. In one incident, a graduate student had to remove a picture of his wife in a bikini because it offended someone else. Then there's the case of Jerold Mackenzie, a manager at the Miller Brewing Co., who one morning discussed a racy episode of *Seinfeld* with a co-worker. After she complained, he was—despite a good record—fired. He was unemployed for two years before suing and winning a $24.7-million judgment against Miller.

Being vague, harassment law becomes a channel for all manner of personal or workplace grievances. In real life, these disputes are as messy as human nature. The *Washington Post* poll also asked how often a "woman falsely files a lawsuit or complaint against a man." Even among women respondents, 34 percent said this happened "often" and 44 percent "sometimes." Of the complaints made to the Equal Employment Opportunity Commission, 40 percent are judged to have "no reasonable cause" and another 40 percent lapse—often because the complainants provide no supporting evidence.

Good laws must be clear. Otherwise people can't obey them and can construe conduct they dislike to be illegal. By this common-sense standard, sexual harassment is horrendously bad law. Worse, the courts have deputized companies to police it because, if they don't, they face lawsuits. To avoid suits, the temptation is to define harassment broadly. At best, firms will increasingly intrude on the speech and private behavior of their workers; at worst, there will be vigilantes in the workplace.

Do we want to go down this path? Clinton's scandal teaches that harassment charges, once made, acquire a momentum of their own. Congress ought to rescue the Supreme Court from its confusion by legislating limits. This seems unlikely. Clinton haters may suspect that the harassment laws are too loose but relish the chance to attack the president; Clinton supporters think the Jones case was used politically but are ideologically committed to broad notions of harassment. The result is a conspiracy of silence—in favor of a lousy law.

The Washington Post
August 12, 1998

STUPID STUDENTS, SMART ECONOMY?

The computer guru at *Newsweek*'s Washington bureau (where I work) graduated from the College of William and Mary in 1983 with a major in English lit without ever using a computer. He acquired his computer skills gradually, first at an editing job elsewhere and then by parlaying that into the *Newsweek* job. I mention all this as a way of asking the obvious question posed by Americans' dismal showing on the international science and math tests: If our students are so bad, why is the economy so good? Among high school seniors, Americans ranked 19 of 21 in math skills. In science, Americans ranked 16 of 21. Even among advanced students (the top 10 to 20 percent), Americans fared poorly. Although Americans were slightly younger than foreign students, the scores were so uniformly low that they can't be dismissed as a fluke.

The main explanation of the paradox is that people don't learn only at school. If they did, we'd be doomed. In isolation, test scores hardly count. What counts—for the economy, at least—is what people do at work. Do they fully use their skills? Do they develop new ones? Are they engaged? Here, the U.S. economy performs better than most. Going back to my pal at *Newsweek,* he developed new skills through job shopping. He found something he does well and enjoys. Among the young, constant job changes often seem aimless and wasteful. In reality, people are usually searching for something that fits their interests and aptitudes. It's better than getting stuck for years in the wrong job.

On the job, people learn from supervisors, mentors, co-workers, customers, and—most important—experience. One Labor Department study estimates that about 70 percent of training in the workplace is informal. Culturally, this is America's strong suit. Tocqueville noted that "Americans are more addicted to practical than theoretical science." Knowledge is often the handmaiden of ambition, not an abstract pleasure. Everyone knows someone (and perhaps lots of someones) who was a lousy student and has done well, often brilliantly, at work.

Compared with European firms, American companies also have greater flexibility to get more from their workers, notes economist Laurie Bassi of the American Society for Training & Development. Our businesses have more freedom to set pay rates, hire and fire, and alter work practices. The results are often decried as unjust: for example, we tolerate huge wage gaps—much larger than in Europe—between high-paid and low-paid workers. To be sure, there are excesses. But mainly, the system succeeds. High wages reward the most productive workers—and entice labor into areas of shortage. Low wages enable the low skilled to get work—and push some to improve their skills.

Because work is learning, the capacity to create work is the capacity to cause learning. Here, too, the U.S. economy excels. French students scored much higher on the international math and science tests than American. But in France, overregulation and high taxes stymie job creation. Only a fifth of the young between 15 and 24 have jobs; in the United States, nearly 60 percent do. Without work, old skills deteriorate and new ones don't develop. Which country does better by its young?

Finally, the economy defies low test scores for two other reasons. First, we overstate the need for advanced science and math skills: a reflection of our high-tech obsession. Economists Anthony Carnevale and Stephen Rose of the Educational Testing Service recently did a study that defined "elite" jobs. These were roughly the top-paying 28 percent of jobs. Most were general managers: personnel directors, purchasing managers, sales executives. They needed math—but not calculus. In 1996, the United States had 1.5 million computer scientists, engineers, and programmers; 1.4 million other engineers; 1 million accountants; 800,000 business financial officers; and 400,000 other scientists (physicists, chemists, etc.). These occupations and a few others defined the population that needs advanced math or science. In a workforce of 132 million, that was 4 percent.

Second, low science and math scores don't mean that all U.S. workplace skills are poor. The Organization for Economic Cooperation and Development has surveyed adult literacy in 12 advanced countries. Americans finish in the middle. We have more superior and more very bad readers than most. The difference between the two studies—one of high school math and science, the other of general literacy—partly reflects what people learn on the job. It also reflects higher U.S. college attendance. In 1995, the college-going rate for those between 15 and 39 was 52 percent in the United States, 33 percent in France, and 27 percent in Germany. Our system offers second, third, and fourth chances.

All this seems reassuring. Indeed, it has caused some commentators to conclude that the international math and science tests are irrelevant. Writing in *The New York Times,* Howard Gardner of the Harvard School of Education dismissed the tests because they measure the "lowest common denominator of facts and skills" and not whether "students can think scientifically or mathematically." This verdict is glib and misleading. Most people can't think sensibly—let alone scientifically—if they don't master basic "facts and skills." If Gardner hadn't learned to write, the *Times* wouldn't have printed his essay.

Schools are one foundation of the economy. If students leave with poor skills, there are consequences. One is waste. Giving people a third or fourth chance (whether in college or on the job) is expensive. Some people learn skills later that they could have learned earlier. And some skills are never learned. One result is scattered scarcities of high-skilled workers; another is many low-skilled workers trapped in poverty or semipermanent unemployment. Some unacquired skills, though unnecessary for jobs, are useful for life. They make us better citizens or parents; they deepen our understanding of the world.

Just because the economy can overcome these failures does not mean that the failures are not real. Low test scores may not be a calamity. But a cause for celebration? Or indifference? Hardly.

The Washington Post
March 12, 1998

ENOUGH BLAME TO GO AROUND

Americans like to believe that all problems are solvable and all tragedies preventable. The mass murder at Columbine High teaches us otherwise. But even so, we go through the process of assessing blame and seeking solutions, because anything else would seem un-American and because this tragedy (like many others) quickly becomes a political vehicle for agendas and ambitions. Our search for scapegoats, though, promises to disappoint.

The usual suspects have emerged. Guns, of course, top the list. I don't own guns, dislike them, and believe that in an ideal world they would be illegal. But let's get real. The federal government reckons there are 230 million handguns, rifles, shotguns, and machine guns in America. Perhaps 40 percent or slightly less of households have a gun. Does anyone truly think that all these people are social misfits and that, as a practical matter, even handguns can be outlawed? Suppose they were. Would the existing supply vanish? Not likely. Black markets would flourish.

Someone determined and intelligent will get guns—or something. Timothy McVeigh used fertilizer to craft his bomb that killed

168 in Oklahoma City. One paradox of the Columbine tragedy is that it occurred when guns are becoming harder to get and sales seem to be declining. The Brady bill, passed in 1993, required law enforcement agencies to check buyers' backgrounds. Between 1993 and 1997, annual purchases of new guns dropped from 7.8 million to 4.3 million, according to government figures.

Parents also rank high as scapegoats. These parents (it's said or implied) must have raised their children poorly. Or they ignored danger signals. In one boy's room, said the Jefferson County sheriff, a sawed-off shotgun barrel was visible. The parents should have suspected. Maybe. But candid parents will admit to doubts. There are limits to child control.

Last year, the psychologist Judith Rich Harris published a book, *The Nurture Assumption,* that challenged the American faith that parents can shape their children as they please. Although she went too far (denying most parental influence), her central point was correct. Heredity—the innate differences among people—and peer influences play a huge role. Every child is different, and children conceal their lives from parents.

A lot of this is inevitable, and much of it is harmless. Some of it, though, leads to tragedies. Even "good" parents are only human. They practice denial and hope. Perhaps Eric Harris's and Dylan Klebold's parents should have known that their sons' weird behavior marked them as mass murderers. But parents regularly miss, or can't alter, signs of trouble in their children. In 1995, there were 2,227 suicides among those under 20 (about half the number of homicides).

America has long suffered from acts of mass violence. In 1927, Andrew Kehoe, angry over a school tax, set off bombs—including one at a school—that killed 38 children, five adults, and himself. In 1949, Howard Unruh, a World War II veteran, shot 13 people to death. In 1966, Charles Whitman set himself up in a tower at the University of Texas with a rifle and killed 16. What's distinctive now is that students have become shooters.

The other day, the First Lady criticized a media culture that "glorifies violence on TV, in the movies, on the Internet, in songs" and features video games where winning is "based on how many people you kill." The effect, she said, is that "our children become desensitized to violence."

There is probably some truth to this, but it overlooks larger, harder truths. High schools have become more chaotic because we have made them that way. We have wanted everyone to graduate. In 1950, only about half of young adults had completed high school. Even in 1960, the dropout rate was 27 percent. It's now about 11 percent. Students who might have once left because they felt angry or inadequate now stay. Schools have grown bigger and more impersonal. In 1950, almost 25,000 public high schools had 5.7 million students. In 1995, fewer than 24,000 schools had 12.5 million students. Columbine has about 1,800.

There has been a loss of control—and it's not just size. In a superb book (*The World We Created at Hamilton High*), sociologist Gerald Grant of Syracuse University described how one high school changed. In the 1950s, it was white and middle class. There was a dress code. The principal's authority was unquestioned. Discipline problems were few. By the 1970s, the school was racially and economically integrated. Electives had diluted the basic curriculum. Students' "rights" to due process had burgeoned. There was no dress code.

Teachers went on the defensive. "Many began to look the other way, to shrink from a challenge and to avoid bringing a charge because they might not only lose the legal battle, but wind up having to defend themselves," wrote Grant. This legacy endures.

Even if a return to the 1950s were possible—and it isn't—it wouldn't be desirable. The principal at Hamilton High was a petty tyrant. Education was exclusionary, conformity widespread. But the change reflects a wider upheaval. It's not just media fare where boundaries between childhood and adulthood have eroded. Teenagers expect many adult freedoms with few adult burdens. They have jobs, cars, incomes. By and large, society accepts this, gives teens "space," and respects their individuality.

Schools are less protective and more open. They are more mixed economically, racially, and ethnically. Our culture celebrates "diversity" and urges people to feel proud of their differences. But in teenagers—who often are struggling to discover who they are—this may be a formula for tension as well as tolerance. People may exaggerate differences or feel them more acutely.

We search for meaning. But the explanation, if any, of the Columbine slaughter lies at the juncture of the dark side of human nature and the drift of our culture. As adolescence and adulthood blend, so do the problems and tragedies. This is a condition that, though it may be influenced, can't be ended.

The Washington Post
May 3, 1999

JUNK JOURNALISM

The *Philadelphia Inquirer* began a ten-part series last week entitled "America: Who Stole the Dream?," which will attract attention. The thesis is simple: Big Government and Big Business are
relentlessly reducing living standards and job security for most
Americans. The series, by Donald Barlett and James Steele, portrays
living in America as a constant hell for all but the superwealthy. This
seems overdrawn, because it is. It's junk journalism, and the intriguing question is why a reputable newspaper publishes it.

I call it "junk" because it fails the basic test of journalistic integrity and competence: it does not strive for truthfulness, however
impossible that ideal is to attain. It does not seek a balanced picture
of the economy—strengths as well as shortcomings—or an accurate
profile of living standards. Instead, it offers endless stories of people
who have suffered setbacks. Their troubles are supposed to speak
for (and to) everyone.

They don't. Statistics implying lower living standards are contradicted by what people buy or own. Homeownership (65 percent of
households) is near a record. In 1980, 11 percent of households

owned a microwave oven, 87 percent a dishwasher, and 56 percent a dryer; by 1993, those figures were 78 percent, 50 percent, and 68 percent. People buy more because their incomes are higher. (Statistics understate incomes by overstating inflation's effect on "real" wages and salaries.) As for anxiety, it exists—and always will. But America is not clinically depressed. The Gallup poll reports that 66 percent of Americans expect their financial situation to improve in the next year.

The *Inquirer*'s twisted portrait of the economy is not, unfortunately, unique. Earlier this year, *The New York Times* ran a distorted series (which I criticized) on corporate "downsizing." A recent CBS Reports called "Who's Getting Rich? And Why Aren't You?" is another example. Explanations for this sort of shoddy journalism fall into three classes: 1) sensationalism—it sells; 2) ideology—journalists detest the profit motive; and 3) ignorance—they don't know better. Sensationalism and antibusiness bias are old hat, but the larger problem, I think, is ignorance or something akin to it.

Journalism copes awkwardly with the ambiguities of many economic stories. We're most comfortable with scandals, trials, politics, sports, and wars. The conflicts are obvious; moral judgments can often be made; and stories have clean endings. The economy defies such simple theater. The process by which wealth is created is unending and complex. Costs and benefits are commingled. What's bad today may be good tomorrow. What hurts some may help many others. Low inflation is good, but ending high inflation may require something bad: a harsh recession.

The capacity of journalists to recognize such distinctions has grown since 1969, when I first began reporting on the economy. Daily economic stories have improved in quality. But there's one glaring exception to this progress: the nation's top editors. Outside the business press (for example, *The Wall Street Journal*), the people who run newspapers, magazines, and TV news divisions don't know much about the economy—and seem unbothered by their ignorance.

The assumption is that most economic stories are done by specialized reporters and aimed at specialized audiences. While this assumption holds, editorial ignorance doesn't matter much. Little damage occurs if know-nothing editors don't do much. But on big projects—newspaper series, magazine cover stories, TV documentaries—the assumption collapses. Editorial control shifts upward, and there's a scramble for familiar news formulas. Editors want villains and heroes, victims and predators. Reporters who promise simple morality tales can sell their stories. The frequent result is journalistic trash.

The *Inquirer* series blames the "global economy" and "free trade" policies for lowering wages and destroying jobs. What it doesn't say is that the trade balance and employment are hardly connected. Barlett and Steele deplore the fact that the last U.S. trade surplus was in 1975; but they don't tell readers that the unemployment rate in 1975 was 8.5 percent. They note that other countries run trade surpluses. Between 1980 and 1995, Germany had 16 annual surpluses, the Netherlands 14, and Sweden 13. But they don't say that the unemployment rates for these countries are 9 percent for Germany, 6 percent for the Netherlands, and 9 percent for Sweden. By contrast, the U.S. rate is 5.1 percent.

Trade doesn't determine unemployment, because trade mainly affects a small part of the job base: manufacturing. In 1995, its share of all U.S. jobs was 16 percent. Trade creates some jobs and destroys others, but total employment depends mainly on the economy's overall vitality. The United States runs regular trade deficits in part because the rest of the world wants dollars to finance global commerce or substitute for weak local currencies. As a result, we don't have to sell as much abroad as we buy; the difference is made up by the dollars that other countries keep. All those extra imports raise—not lower—U.S. living standards.

If Barlett and Steele wanted to inform readers, they'd explain all this. Maybe they will in later installments, though it's doubtful. They're mainly interested in condemning. Everything they discuss (trade policies, growing income inequality, executive compensation) is the legitimate stuff of journalism. What's illegitimate is to report matters so selectively—with so little attention to conflicting evidence or any larger context—that ordinary readers are misled. The press can do better. The *Los Angeles Times* recently ran a good series on the gains that economic change creates as well as the trauma it inflicts.

The real fault here lies with the top editors (at the *Inquirer,* the *Times,* and other media giants) who commission or approve these distortions. There's no excuse for their ineptness. The "economic story" is no longer new. It is central to the American condition and, therefore, a permanent concern of journalism. If editors don't understand the economy, they can't exercise good judgment. The present sanctioned stupidity leads to junk journalism.

Newsweek
September 23, 1996

SEX, SPIN, AND CIRCULATION

The clean little secret about teenage sex is that there's less of it than there used to be: not much less, but enough to reverse a long upward spiral. You would not have learned this, however, from *Time* magazine's recent cover story: "Everything Your Kids Already Know about Sex." Teens know more about sex than ever, it said. So there must be (it implied) more teen sex than ever. The first notion may be true; the second isn't.

Surveys by the National Center for Health Statistics show that teenage sexual activity has declined in the 1990s. In 1995, the proportion of girls 15 to 19 who had ever had sex was 50 percent, down from 53 percent in 1988 and 55 percent in 1990. That ended years of rises: in 1970, only 29 percent of teen girls had had sex. Boys showed a similar drop. The frequency of sex may also be declining. Among boys, 38 percent had had sex within three months of the survey in 1995; in 1988, the figure was 43 percent.

We in the press prize a reputation for honesty, and when one of us falsifies, we get huffy. There has been much of this lately. Stephen Glass, a writer for the *New Republic,* was revealed to have invented sources. Patricia Smith, a *Boston Globe* columnist, resigned after fabricating people and quotes. But lying is a rare sin. The more common problem—less noted—is selective or sloppy reporting of the type in the *Time* story. The facts and quotes may be correct, but the overall message is questionable or wrong.

Time isn't alone. Almost any reporter with a long career (me included; also note, I write for *Newsweek*) has erred sometimes. *The Wall Street Journal* recently said, in a review of public opinion, that "the defining political issue of the 1990s is health care" and cited mass unhappiness with managed care. Well, maybe. But after reviewing polls on health care, Karlyn Bowman of the American Enterprise Institute concluded that discontent is overstated. For example, Gallup regularly asks people to rate the nation's biggest problem. The April results were the budget deficit, 5 percent; health care, 6 percent; the economy, 11 percent; crime, 20 percent.

"The secret of our business—first, you simplify; then, you exaggerate," an unknown newsman once said. Deadline pressure is a worn, yet often true, excuse for mistakes. Other causes are weaker. How about ambition? Most reporters crave the big story. How about commercial pressure? Powerful media empires threaten journalistic integrity less than new sources of news—cable TV, the Internet. Editors face fierce competition for people's attention. Everyone needs hot stories to boost circulation and TV ratings, which draw advertising. Packaging (covers, headlines, pictures, and prose) becomes everything; spin is in. Truth gets pinched.

I suspect—but can't prove—that this sort of climate encouraged *Time*'s cover on teenage sex. It instantly got my attention, because I have a 13-year-old daughter (and also sons 11 and 8). She avidly watches one of the TV shows featured in the story, *Dawson's Creek,* a series in which, among other things, a high school student has an affair with one of his teachers. *Time* then leaps from more TV teen sex to more real teen sex.

Although the story never states this directly—it can't without hard evidence—it suggests the connection in many ways. The story opens with a four-column picture of two teens, partially disrobed and sprawled on each other, with his hand creeping toward her fanny. The story's first four pull-quotes (highlighted in big type) emphasize the ease of real sex:

"If you're feeling steamy and hot, there's only one thing you want to do."—Stephanie, who lost her virginity at age 14.

"If the President can do it, why can't we?"—a male student, reasoning at a Denver middle school.

"Teens today are almost nonchalant about sex."—junior high school counselor in Salt Lake City.

"If you watch TV, they've got everything you want to know."—Brett, 14, in Denver.

The story's writer, Ron Stodghill II, said he knew of surveys showing less teenage sex but minimized the drops because they occurred from levels much higher than in the early 1970s (true). He emphasized "how kids are bombarded with sexual images" and how parents have less influence over their behavior. Halfway through, the story briefly mentions that the teenage birthrate is down 12 percent since 1991—a fact attributed to more contraception. The story's editor, Howard Chua-Eoan, said he didn't know that surveys showed less sex; Stodghill said he was told.

Whatever happened, the story was misleading. "Those are real kids in the story," said Kristin Moore of Child Trends, which monitors children's issues. But "there's also the other extreme—fundamentalist kids who take chastity vows." And many teens are in the middle. They feel awkward, hesitant, or fearful toward early sex. Surveys confirm this muddled picture.

Some teens are having sex earlier than ever. Between 1988 and 1995, the proportion of girls having sex before age 15 rose from 11 to 19 percent, report Joyce Abma of the National Center for Health Statistics and Freya Sonenstein of the Urban Institute. Not all this sex is voluntary. Some is rape. Some is so compelled that girls later judge it "unwanted." By contrast, the broader decline in teen sex is concentrated in the suburbs. Among suburban girls 15 to 19, the proportion who had had sex within three months of the survey dropped from 41 to 34 percent between 1988 and 1995. In central cities, there was little change.

We can't fully explain these trends. Isabel Sawhill of the National Campaign to Prevent Teen Pregnancy says that the fear of AIDS deters teens. She also suspects that values are shifting. A poll of college freshmen asks whether "sex is okay if people like each other." In 1987, 52 percent thought so; by 1996, only 42 percent did. And parents may matter: in families with two biological parents, teen sex (at age 15) occurs half as often as in one-parent families. If children feel more secure or loved, they may be less vulnerable, adventurous, or foolish.

Time's story offended me as a parent and reporter. It falsely told teens that everyone's "doing it"—or soon will—when everyone isn't. Peer pressure based on bad information isn't likely to lead to good decisions. The story was a fine read but achieved spin at the expense of truth.

The Washington Post
July 1, 1998

GATES ISN'T GOD
(OR EVEN HENRY FORD)

Gates has "achieved an unprecedented, and still growing,
impact on the civilized world."

Newsweek
August 18, 1997

Bill Gates isn't God—not yet. Every so often, the media anoint
some business figure with mythical powers. Gates has now
achieved this status. Jules Feiffer caught the mood in a recent cartoon titled "Bill Gates Visits the Grand Canyon." Gates is peering
into the canyon, and the canyon thinks: "He makes me feel so in-
significant." But the canyon will still be there when Gates is gone
and long forgotten. The obsession with Gates says more about our
faddishness than it does about his place in history.

Gates is his own best promoter. It's hard to escape him, whether
he's chatting with Tom Brokaw or letting *Time* editor Walter Isaac-
son glimpse his personal life ("In Search of the Real Bill Gates,"
cover story January 13) or granting a long Q&A to *Newsweek* ("How
We Did It," June 23). Aside from sheer vanity or a desire to philoso-
phize, Gates's openness probably reflects self-interest. Given Microsoft's power, he knows that it will be scrutinized constantly for
antitrust violations. He seeks to project a low-key and even folksy
image—in a geekish way—to counter criticism that he's terrorizing
the computer industry.

To say (as *Newsweek* does) that his impact has been "unprecedented" is, strictly speaking, true. We're all unique; my impact is unprecedented, and so is yours. Otherwise the statement is silly. Astonishing though the PC may be, its social significance still falls short of that of many past technologies: the railroad (which created a national market); the automobile (which transformed living and working patterns); the TV (which became the greatest form of mass entertainment); and antibiotics (which tamed many deadly infections). And there was the harnessing of electricity itself in the late nineteenth century.

Even if the PC were now in a league with these, Microsoft has made none of its critical technical advances. These started with the invention of the transistor in the late 1940s and then of the integrated circuit in 1957. In 1971, Intel developed the microprocessor, the "brains" of the personal computer. Apple popularized the notion that the personal computer was something for everyone. The icons that appear on computer screens were conceived by Xerox and commercialized by Apple.

Gates has been a brilliant opportunist. He benefited from one of the biggest business blunders of modern times: IBM's oversight in not buying the operating system (MS-DOS) for its personal computer in 1981. Instead it left Microsoft the exclusive rights to this software, which holds the computer's basic instructions. As IBM cloning mushroomed, Gates had a license to print money. And Microsoft didn't even write the original DOS program, which was purchased for $75,000 from another small start-up firm.

None of this dims Gates's business skills. It was not preordained that Microsoft ascend while other companies (IBM, Digital Equipment, Apple) stumble. Microsoft might have lost its quasi monopoly. At one point, IBM created an alternative operating system (OS/2); it flopped. Apple's mistakes removed it as a major rival. Microsoft crafted contracts with PC makers to deter competition. Hardware companies often paid a licensing fee for each computer, even if it didn't use MS-DOS.

This protected "the DOS monopoly," write Stephen Manes and Paul Andrews in *Gates*. "If you were already paying a [royalty to Microsoft] on every machine . . . you weren't likely to offer a different operating system." (The practice was banned in a 1994 antitrust consent decree with the Justice Department.)

But Gates's business triumphs do not yet qualify him as an innovator in the mold of, say, Edison or Ford. Ford is the best comparison, and the similarities—and differences—are revealing. Both were early enthusiasts for a new technology. Ford tinkered in a woodshed to build his first car in 1896; Gates wrote software as a teenager. Ford didn't personally invent any critical technical improvement to the car; as noted, the story is similar for Gates and the computer. What separates the two is that Ford pioneered a system of mass production that altered all industry and the face of America.

Before the Model T in 1908, cars were costly and scarce. Ford's decision to make only one model and his streamlining of production—including the adoption of the assembly line—changed that. Between 1908 and 1913, Ford's output went from 10,202 cars to 202,667; by 1923, it was 1.8 million. His approach was widely copied. By contrast, the PC explosion has been driven by the growing power of chips to make computers more versatile and user-friendly. Microsoft may have slightly speeded the process by creating a dominant and recognizable software that hastened consumer acceptance. But it would still have proceeded rapidly, as the Internet shows. Gates was late to see its importance; it grew anyway.

The point is not to vilify, or deify, Gates. His financial power is unquestioned. Every business craves a product monopoly and rapid growth. Microsoft has both. In the 1990s, global PC sales have risen 20 percent annually, says Dataquest. More than 90 percent of the world's 250 million PCs run on MS-DOS or its successor, Windows. Microsoft has $9 billion in cash, despite $1.9 billion in annual R&D spending and some costly acquisitions, including $1 billion for 11.5 percent of Comcast, a cable TV operator. It also said it would buy

WebTV Networks—whose technology allows TVs to use the Internet—for $425 million.

Nor is the point to settle the raging debate about whether Gates is an energetic visionary or a predatory competitor. A case can be made for either. Two-thirds of Microsoft's business now is in competitive software markets. Microsoft gives away some key programs (example: its Internet browser, Explorer) to gain market share. But Gates's constant striving—now apparently aimed at marrying the computer and TV—maintains pressure for change.

The more modest message is that the Gates stereotype is a stretch. He is not single-handedly remaking society. Using the Internet instead of the phone to buy a plane ticket is a change, not a revolution. What makes his story so American and so compelling is the relentlessness of his enthusiasm and the rawness of his ambition. He seems more like Vince Lombardi than Thomas Edison. "Winning isn't everything," Lombardi said. "It's the only thing." Gates brings that credo to cyberspace.

The Washington Post
August 27, 1997

REQUIEM FOR THE TYPEWRITER

It was inevitable. Sooner or later, the last great name in American typewriters was bound to self-destruct, bringing to a formal conclusion something that had long ago ended. It happened last week with the bankruptcy of Smith Corona, which once produced manual portable typewriters that were hauled off to college and elsewhere by millions of Americans, including me. In the office next to mine sits a summer college intern busily tapping at his Macintosh PowerBook (nobody ever "bangs" at a laptop). That's what killed the typewriter.

Just for the record, this column is being written on an old Royal manual. In the combat between computers and typewriters, my loyalties lie with the losers. For writing, the typewriter still has advantages over a computer. Writing is the grinding process of discovering the right flow of words to convey a story, feeling, explanation, or argument. Mistakes, false starts, and revisions are not only inevitable. They are essential. You need them. A phrase that didn't fit at ten in the morning may, by three in the afternoon, be exactly what you need.

The virtue of the typewriter is that it saves my blunders. I rip out my incoherent drafts and spread them across my desk, where I scavenge for serviceable phrases. The typewriter's other appeal is that it compels me to rewrite by making me retype. Every rewrite suggests some superior word or exposes some sloppy construction. No doubt, computers can deliver similar benefits. Drafts can be printed. But why bother? The typewriter is simpler. I am not utterly hostile to the computer. Once the main composing is complete, I punch my draft into an old IBM PC, which makes the final editing much easier.

By last week, of course, all these issues had been decisively settled against the typewriter. The quality of writing may not have advanced with the computer, but the ease of "processing" and printing words surely has. Gibberish can quickly be made to look neat and impressive. Smith Corona's bankruptcy was merely a symbolic benchmark. The company may ultimately emerge from bankruptcy, and a few other typewriter makers survive. Still, the traditional typewriter is dead.

Its passing deserves notice. What is worth recalling is that, in its time, the typewriter was every bit as revolutionary as today's computer. It was a great feat of design and manufacturing that transformed work and women's role in society. As with most great inventions, its commercial birth was slow and hard. The first modern typewriter was built in 1867 by a Milwaukee inventor named Christopher Latham Sholes. It was also Sholes who devised today's universal keyboard (qwerty).

Early typewriters succeeded technically and failed financially. Production costs were too high. Output didn't soar until the late 1880s, after manufacturing rights had been sold to another company. Economic historian Donald Hoke says the typewriter was "the most complex mechanism mass produced by American industry" in the nineteenth century because (as one factory manager said) "its thousands of parts must work together with exquisite exactness, yet withstand hard usage."

Mark Twain was a pioneer. "It piles an awful stack of words on one page. It don't muss things or scatter ink blots around," he wrote to his brother in 1874. Twain submitted the first typewritten book manuscript to a publisher. He identified it as "Tom Sawyer" (1876), though some historians think he erred and the distinction belongs to "Life on the Mississippi" (1883). But the typewriter's largest impact was on women and the American office, which was until the late nineteenth century a male bastion.

Consider. In 1870, men constituted 98 percent of all clerical workers. Most took dictation, copied documents, or ran errands. By 1920, half the clerical workers were women. The typewriter had created a demand for literate workers that could be easily filled only by women who—in the nineteenth century—outnumbered men among high school graduates. Schools were established for typists, who numbered 615,000 by 1920. Although these jobs were later stigmatized as oppressing women, they were initially liberating. Until then, teaching had been the only job outlet for educated women. And typists' pay was attractive: in the 1890s, $6 to $15 a week compared with $1.50 to $8 for factory workers.

The typewriter is unappreciated because it has always been overshadowed by more imposing technologies. At the turn of the century, there was the telephone, electric light, and automobile. Now there is the computer. I do feel guilty that I am not fully participating—wow, that's a wild understatement—in the great technology event of our time. The feeling fades, though, whenever *Newsweek*'s computer system crashes or I hear someone complaining about the tedium of learning a new "word processing" program, whose purported advances have zip to do with writing.

Computers can, of course, provide vast amounts of information. Databases and documents can be downloaded; Web sites can be accessed. (I'm flaunting my computer jargon here.) But getting information has never been my problem; the hard part is deciding what it means. Among computer enthusiasts, I have not detected any increase in knowledge or wisdom. Mainly, they seem to have more time to waste buzzing around cyberspace. At home, my wife and children have a more powerful machine than my original IBM PC, which is all I truly need. I keep waiting for something that will entice me to become a computer buff.

Until then, I'm sticking with my Royal. It won't give me e-mail. But I don't want e-mail. Nor will it play games when I ought to write. Good. Getting parts is a problem. My local repair shop recently closed. I've now found a new one about 20 miles away that, although it handles mostly electronic machines, will still fix manuals. The manager tells me on the phone that there aren't many manual customers left. Well, there's one more coming.

Newsweek
July 17, 1995

A LIFE'S LESSON

THE GIFT OF A GREAT TEACHER

If you are lucky in life, you will have at least one great teacher. More than three decades ago, I had Ed Banfield, a political scientist who taught mainly at the University of Chicago and Harvard University. Ed's recent death at 83 saddened me (which was expected) and left me with a real sense of loss (which wasn't). Although we had stayed in touch, we were never intimate friends or intellectual soulmates. The gap between us in intellectual candlepower was too great. But he had loomed large in my life, and I have been puzzling why his death has so affected me.

I think the answer—and the reason for writing about something so personal—goes to the heart of what it means to be a great teacher. By teacher, I am not referring primarily to classroom instructors, because learning in life occurs mainly outside of schools. I first encountered Ed in a lecture hall, but his greatness did not lie in giving good lectures (which he did). It lay instead in somehow transmitting life-changing lessons. If I had not known him, I would be a different person. He helped me become who I am and, more important, who I want to be.

When you lose someone like that, there is a hole. It is a smaller hole than losing a parent, a child, or close friend. But it is still a hole, because great teachers are so rare. I have, for example, worked for some very talented editors. A few have earned my lasting gratitude for improving my reporting or writing. But none has been a great teacher; none has changed my life.

What gave Ed this power was, first, his ideas. He made me see new things or old things in new ways. The political scientist James Q. Wilson—first Ed's student, then his collaborator—has called Banfield the most profound student of American politics in this century. Although arguable, this is surely plausible.

Americans take democracy, freedom, and political stability for granted. Ed was more wary. These great things do not exist in isolation. They must somehow fuse into a political system that fulfills certain essential social functions: to protect the nation; to provide some continuity in government and policy; to maintain order and modulate society's most passionate conflicts. The trouble, Ed believed, is that democracies have certain self-destructive tendencies and that, in modern America, these had intensified.

On the whole, he regretted the disappearance after World War II of a political system based on big-city machines (whose supporters were rewarded with patronage jobs and contracts) and on party bosses (who dictated political candidates from city council to Congress and, often, the White House). It was not that he favored patronage, corruption, or bosses for their own sake. But in cities, they created popular support for government and gave it the power to accomplish things. And they emphasized material gain over ideological fervor.

Postwar suburbanization and party reforms—weakening bosses and machines—destroyed this system. Its replacement, Ed feared, was inferior. Whereas the old system had promised personal rewards, he wrote, the new one promises social reform. Politicians would now merchandise themselves by selling false solutions to exaggerated problems. The politician, like the TV news commentator, must always have something to say even when nothing urgently needs to be said, he wrote in 1970. By several decades, this anticipated the term *talking head.* People would lose respect for government because many solutions would fail. Here, too, he anticipated. Later, polls showed dropping public confidence in national leaders. Ed was not surprised.

He taught that you had to understand the world as it is, not as you wished it to be. This was sound advice for an aspiring reporter. And Ed practiced it. In 1954 and 1955, he and his wife, Laura (they would ultimately be married 61 years), spent time in a poor Italian village to explain its poverty. The resulting book—*The Moral Basis of a Backward Society*—remains a classic. Families in the village, it argued, so distrusted each other that they could not cooperate to promote common prosperity. The larger point (still missed by many economists) is that local culture, not just markets, determines economic growth.

What brought Ed fleeting prominence—notoriety, really—was *The Unheavenly City.* Published in 1970, it foretold the failure of the War on Poverty. Prosperity, government programs, and less racial discrimination might lift some from poverty, he said. But the worst problems of poverty and the cities would remain. They resulted from a lower class whose members were so impulsive and present-oriented that they attached no value to work, sacrifice, self-improvement, or service to family, friends, or community. They dropped out of school, had illegitimate children, and were unemployed. Government couldn't easily alter their behavior.

For this message, Ed was reviled as a reactionary. He repeatedly said that most black Americans didn't belong to the lower class and that it contained many whites. Still, many dismissed him as a racist. Over time, his theories gained some respectability from the weight of experience. Poverty defied government assaults; his lower class was relabeled "the underclass." But when he wrote, Ed was assailing prevailing opinion. He knew he would be harshly, even viciously, attacked. He wrote anyway and endured the consequences.

This was the deeper lesson. Perhaps all great teachers—whether parents, bosses, professors, or whoever—ultimately convey some moral code. Ed surely did. What he was saying in the 1960s was not what everyone else was saying. I felt uneasy with the reigning orthodoxy. But I didn't know why. Ed helped me understand my doubts and made me feel that it was important to give them expression. The truth had to be pursued, no matter how inconvenient, unpopular, unfashionable, or discomforting. Ed did not teach that; he lived it. This was his code, and it was—for anyone willing to receive it—an immeasurable gift.

Newsweek
October 18, 1999

Acknowledgments

Unlike (perhaps) some writers, I regard editors as my allies. If they don't understand what I'm trying to say, chances are that no one else will, either. They constantly make me look better than I am. Joel Havemann, my best friend, has edited my non-*Newsweek* columns for years. He has consistently compelled me to complete incomplete thoughts and has nudged me away from my own worst instincts. Alan Shearer runs the Washington Post Writers Group, and his cheerful doggedness forced me—mostly against my will—to sign up in 1996. It was one of the best decisions I never made. Working with Alan is a delight. He has more confidence in my work than I do and is an endless source of suggestions and new ideas.

At *Newsweek,* the present editor, Mark Whitaker, has been consistently supportive of the tone and perspective I add to the magazine. A number of business editors (in addition to Mark, who once held the job) have helped sharpen my copy: Lewis Dvorkin, Hank Gilman, Mark Vamos, and the present editor, Eben Shapiro. Mel Elfin, the former Washington bureau chief, was instrumental in bringing me to *Newsweek:* a move that leaves me forever in his debt. In the Washington bureau, where I have worked since 1984, Rich Thomas has not only been a good friend but also a relentless prod to thought and reporting. Rich—a superb reporter and a shrewd judge of human nature—has more ideas in a day than most people have in a year. I have shamelessly plagiarized many of his best. Although there are no columns here from my days at *National Journal*—many are too dated—the magazine's recently retired editor, Richard

Frank, set a high standard of journalistic competence and integrity that benefited all those privileged to work with him.

Putting together this collection would not have been possible without the help of others. Kevin Lamb of *Newsweek*'s Washington library retrieved all my past columns from electronic archives, as well as responding to a variety of other requests. He has my lasting thanks. He and Lucy Shackelford, who heads the library, are incredibly competent in getting facts, figures, documents, articles, and books for those of us in the bureau. At Random House, Janelle Duryea navigated me through the production process without any major calamities. Jon Karp—who recently left Random House as a senior editor—decided to publish this collection. I appreciate his confidence. My agent, Rafe Sagalyn, is tireless in his patience with my quirks; for his troubles, he hasn't earned much except my gratitude.

My wife and children must often wonder what I do all day (I know I do). This collection may convince them that I don't do much. I would dedicate it to them, except that they received the dedication of my first book and most of my life is dedicated to them, anyway. So this goes to Richard, the smarter and funnier brother. I'm lucky he decided to go into another line of work.

About the Author

ROBERT J. SAMUELSON writes a regular column for *Newsweek* and the Washington Post Writers Group. He began his career in journalism as a reporter for *The Washington Post* in 1969. After leaving the *Post* in 1973, he did freelance writing until mid-1976, when he joined the *National Journal* magazine as an economics correspondent and columnist. The *Post* began using his *National Journal* column in 1977; in 1984, he left the *National Journal* for *Newsweek*. He lives in Bethesda, Maryland, with his wife, Judy Herr, and their three children, Ruth, Michael, and John.

AtRandom.com books are original publications that make their first public appearance in the world as e-books, followed by a trade paperback edition. AtRandom.com books are timely and topical. They exploit new technologies, such as hyper-links, multimedia enhancements, and sophisticated search functions. Most of all, they are consumer-powered, providing readers with choices about their reading experience.

AtRandom.com books are aimed at highly defined communities of motivated readers who want immediate access to substantive and artful writing on the various subjects that fascinate them.

Our list features literary journalism; fiction; investigative reporting; cultural criticism; short biographies of entertainers, athletes, moguls, and thinkers; examinations of technology and society; and practical advice. Whether written in a spirit of play or rigorous critique, these books possess a vitality and daring that new ways of publishing can aptly serve.

For information about AtRandom.com Books and to sign up for our e-newsletters, visit www.atrandom.com.